Dance N

A Guide to Musical Referenc ....ny Powell's
A Dance to the Music of Time

Jeffrey Manley
with
Nicholas Birns, Edwin Bock
John Gould, Paul Guinery
Peter Kislinger and Prue Raper

Introduction by Paul Guinery

Anthony Powell Society : Greenford, UK
2010

First published in 2010 by The Anthony Powell Society,
76 Ennismore Avenue, Greenford, Middlesex, UB6 0JW, UK

ISBN 978-0954173661

Printed by Lonsdale Print Services, Wellingborough, UK

This book is written in commemoration of the
50th anniversary of the publication of
Casanova's Chinese Restaurant
and the introduction of the characters of
Hugh Moreland and his friends into the novels
of Anthony Powell

Contents

Editorial Foreword

This Guide to musical references in Anthony Powell's novel sequence, *A Dance to the Music of Time,* was inspired in the first instance by Hilary Spurling's *Invitation to the Dance: A Handbook to Anthony Powell's A Dance to the Music of Time* (London, 1992, previous ed. 1977; Boston, 1978) (hereafter "*Spurling*"). Any readers of *Dance* who have also used *Spurling* will appreciate how their enjoyment of the novels has been enhanced by that experience. While *Spurling* has detailed references to characters, books, paintings, and places mentioned in *Dance*, it offers no similar detailed discussion of musical references (although there are helpful abbreviated references to Popular Music and Hymns in the Book section which provided the starting point for many of the entries in this Guide on those topics).

As will be seen from the entries in this Guide, the musical references in *Dance* are no less (or only slightly less) numerous than those for the non-character topics covered by *Spurling*. Anyone wishing to secure more detailed knowledge of these references and their relationship to each other can use this Guide as a supplement to *Spurling*. To that end, we have structured this Guide to be consistent with *Spurling* with as few changes as possible.

One difference that should be noted is that, in this Guide, we have used material published by Powell in his memoirs, journals and notebook most of which were not available when *Spurling* was written. In addition, character entries fall into three categories: (1) professional musicians or those who make their living through music (such as Moreland, Maclintick *etc.*) each have individual entries under their names; (2) "street musicians" and (3) "music lovers, amateur performers and patrons". Moreover, character entries are limited to the musical associations of these characters, most of whom will also have more general references in *Spurling*.

All references both to characters and fictional musical compositions are marked by a double asterisk. Similarly, places are only referred to in connection with their musical associations. References to pre- and post-*Dance* novels are included where they relate to *Dance* entries and were known to the editors, but no attempt at systematic identification of musical references in these other works has been attempted. Otherwise, the approach to the organization and content of the entries should be familiar to a user of *Spurling*.

This Guide came about as the result of the encouragement and support given by Keith Marshall, Honorary Secretary of the Anthony Powell Society, and other members of the Society. An editorial group was formed in the summer of 2006. I accepted the responsibility of general editor and most of the non-fictional references were drafted in rough form by me; these, as well as other draft entries were circulated to the entire group for comment. The other members of the group consisted of Nick Birns (who also contributed the entries for Emmanuel Chabrier and Feodor Chaliapin as well as general comments and edits), Ed Bock (who provided comments on various aspects of the draft with particular reference to elimination of superfluous material), John Gould (who drafted the entries on characters and fictional music as well as offering other comments and edits), Peter Kislinger (who provided detailed comments and editorial help, especially on entries relating to opera and classical music), and Prue Raper (who provided detailed comments and edits, especially on hymns and choral music, as well as the service sheets from Powell's Memorial Service and the 1945 Victory Thanksgiving Service in St Paul's Cathedral, which are attached as appendices). Keith Marshall provided the service sheet for Powell's funeral (attached as Appendix C) and revised the text for publication.

Finally, Paul Guinery independently organized a splendid performance of selected music from *Dance* which was presented in February 2007 in London just as the first round of work on this Guide was coming to completion. A transcript of that performance is attached as Appendix E. Paul also contributed valuable additions to and edits of the entries on popular music, recordings and performances that are included in many references. Moreover, he also kindly agreed to write the Introduction.

Help was also provided by individual members of the so-called APLIST, an internet discussion group sponsored by the Anthony Powell Society. For example, Patric Dickinson, former Anthony Powell Society Chairman, offered information on the enigmatic Varda based on research he had done for a presentation at the Society's Annual General Meeting for 2009. Helplines from other internet sites also offered information on questions not answered by the usual research materials. These included sites for individual composers (*eg.* Albert Lortzing and Ralph Vaughan Williams) as well as research establishments such as the Imperial War Museum which offered helpful suggestions regarding soldiers' songs. The musical reference staffs of both the British Library and the Library of Congress also provided valuable assistance and suggestions. And last but certainly not least, the British Music Hall Society and its members provided information available nowhere else on songs beloved of Ted Jeavons such as his recitation of "I ran a pin in Gwendolyn" which was identified by BMHS member David Paramor from memory of a recorded version on a 78 rpm record in his collection.

Most of the research was based on secondary sources on the internet (such as Wikipedia, Cyberhymnal, Oremus, IMDb, IBDb, Mudcat *etc.*). More specialized sites for individual composers or musical genres were also consulted. For example, some songs have their own internet pages – *eg. John Peel, The Ash Grove, Kashmiri Song*. British Army bugle calls also have an internet site. Printed sources such as the *New Grove Dictionary of Music, The*

Penguin Book of Hymns and other printed musical reference works as well as monographs on individual composers and performers were also consulted. In order to simplify the text, these are cited only where necessary.

I have tried to check all entries against a second or third source, but in some cases this was not possible. To the extent that there are errors, they are mine, and corrections would be appreciated so as to enable their inclusion in future editions. One day it is hoped to have a comprehensive reference guide to *Dance* (which is one of the stated goals of the Anthony Powell Society), and this Guide is intended as a source for the annotations on musical references.

Abbreviations and page references for the *Dance* novels follow the format of *Spurling.* [See *Spurling,* note, *xx.*] Articles at the beginning of any reference in any language (the, *le, der etc.*) are not considered in determining placement in alphabetical listings. In addition, page references to Powell's memoirs, journals, notebook and non-*Dance* novels follow the pagination of the London first editions (except as noted below). Abbreviations of those works are as follows:

Infants	*Infants of the Spring* (1976)
Messengers	*Messengers of Day* (1978)
Faces	*Faces in My Time* (1980)
Strangers	*The Strangers All Are Gone* (1982)
J82-86	*Journals: 1982-1986* (1995)
J87-89	*Journals: 1987-1989* (1996)
J90-92	*Journals: 1990-1993* (1997)
AM	*Afternoon Men* (London, 1974 reprint)
A&P	*Agents and Patients* (London, 1973 reprint)
FK	*The Fisher King* (1986)
FVD	*From a View to a Death* (London, 1972 reprint)
V	*Venusberg* (London, 1977 reprint)
Wheel	*O, How the Wheel Becomes It* (1983)
WBW	*What's Become of Waring* (London, 1973 reprint)
WN	*A Writer's Notebook* (2000)

Jeffrey Manley
June 2010

Introduction

"Strange, how potent"

More years ago than I usually own up to, I fell in love for the first time. I was a 19-year-old student; my beloved was a mature lady already in her mid-fifties. My Dante-esque vision of this alluring Beatrice came initially as through a glass darkly, when I glimpsed her standing in the dingy window of an Oxford antique shop. She was deeply tanned in colouring, just four feet tall, with small shapely legs and, like the fabled bandit, one-armed – in this case a limb surprisingly fat and metallic. Upon further acquaintance she would prove eloquent in speech and music but would need careful handling.

She was, in fact, a gramophone. Or to be coldly statistical, an HMV cabinet model 170 (circa 1923) with a No.2 soundbox allied to a fat tone-arm with tapering gooseneck. She was also well-endowed with a quadruple-spring motor. Upon enquiry, it came as no surprise that such a desirable partner had little intention of selling herself cheaply. In order to possess her, fifty pounds was required.

It was a lot of money for me then and it took most of a university term to scrape together. In the meantime I hardly dared pass the shop-window where she held court in case another suitor had called and had had the presumption to elope with her. But finally I amassed the fee and claimed her for my own, though not without spending what the French call *un mauvais quart d'heure*: the handle with which to wind the clockwork innards of this sleeping beauty and bring her to life could not at first be found. Her guardian behind the counter was infuriatingly off-hand; but I was firm and insisted, successfully, on a proper search. So it was a proud moment when my "best-man" (a friend bribed with a pint in the college beer-cellar) helped me carry model 170 across the threshold of my digs. It was the start of a beautiful friendship. Thirty years later, I love her still – even more so, now that she is in her dignified eighties. She wears well but then I have not neglected her and, in any case, she has always been a working-girl. As an admonitory notice in her hand-book cautions: "<u>dis</u>use is bad for the machine".

It wasn't, at that time, difficult to find second-hand 78 rpm records: bric-a-brac shops would virtually give them away. I soon amassed a sizeable collection, ranging from earthy ditties of the Edwardian music-hall ("Look What Percy's Picked Up In The Park", as Miss Vesta Victoria insisted on revealing); poignant farewells from doomed 1914 "Tommies" ("Hark, I hear the bugle calling, Goodbye Dolly Gray"); Charlestons and Black-Bottoms from the dizzy 'Twenties along with their collegiate equivalent, the "Varsity Drag" (whatever that was – though according to the enthused vocalist "everybody" was exhaustively "doing it"); jazz-bands with names such as The

Sparkling Syncopators or (my favourite) The Clicquot Club Eskimos; haunting show-tunes of the 1930s ("I'm on a see-saw: you throw me up and you throw me down, I don't know whether I'm here or there", warbled by a justifiably bemused John Mills).

Later, whenever I played such gems of the shellac recording industry to members of an older generation, the response was positively startling: a prim maiden-aunt would suddenly seize a feather-duster to give a passable imitation of Binnie Hale as a 1930s parlour-maid, shamelessly gloating that she'd taken to drink ("I like a nice cup of tea in the morning, for to start the day, you see ... and when it's time for bed, there's a lot to be said for a nice cup of tea"); whilst a bachelor uncle, of the pipe-smoking variety, was galvanized into quoting the entire refrain and (even more impressively) the verse of the title song from *No, No Nanette* ("sometime perhaps you'll have your way, when you are old and turning grey, but just as yet it's always no! no! no! Nanette!"), recalling thespian ambitions as a chorus-boy in the 1939 revival ("French's Acting Edition") by the National Provincial Bank's Amateur Dramatic Society ("costumes and wigs on hire from Messrs Charles H Fox Ltd of High Holborn, WC1").

For total recall, it undoubtedly was. Unnervingly accurate in terms of lyrics and music, this was the well-known phenomenon of memory effortlessly recapturing the debris of fifty years ago whilst struggling with that of five weeks previous. The benefits of this extraordinary gift from the Gods are especially fruitful in the case of popular music, itself so evocative of a given period and so effective in functioning as a time-machine to the past. It is not surprising that such music has a role to play in literature as well. No wonder novelists like Anthony Powell picked up on the technique of Proust who himself extended, in a musical analogy, his concept of the *madeleine* dipped in lime-tea to recapture *le temps perdu*. The so-called "*petite phrase*" of Proust's novel-sequence is an aural *aide-mémoire* that can be equally as significant as a gastronomic one in cheating Time.

Writers from an earlier age than Proust or Powell have also discovered this "strange potency". Lord Byron for example, abroad in Ravenna in 1821, was troubled and moved by it:

> *Oh! There is an organ playing in the street – a waltz too! I must leave off to listen. They are playing a waltz which I have heard ten thousand times at the balls in London ... Music is a strange thing.*

A strange thing but a universal one. For at one time music could also be relied on for what we would now call its "inclusiveness". Just as the toffs mingled at the Music Hall with the workers, so too did different age groups share musical tastes. Newly-minted pop music wasn't the prerogative of teenagers as it largely is today and the latest hit by George Gershwin or

Jerome Kern knew no frontiers of age or class. It is our loss, and perhaps that of future novelists, that contemporary pop music excludes far more than it includes.

My grandmother adored that incomparable artiste and comedienne Gracie Fields and from her I inherited a large collection of 78s which I grew to love. Grandma was in her eighties when we listened with a shared delight to Miss Fields unpacking for us the contents of her "Little Bottom Drawer" or knowingly extolling the dimensions of "The Biggest Aspidistra in the World". It might have seemed bizarre, even unhealthy, for someone in their late twenties, as I was, to have shared an old lady's tastes. But then my grandmother wasn't 83 when she'd first heard those recordings: she'd been more or less the age I was when I was discovering them for the first time. Eventually, familiarity with a style of expression also dissolves the distancing effect of Time and now, having listened to so much popular music from the first half of the 20th century, it no longer sounds particularly "quaint", let alone "old-fashioned", to my ears. In fact it sounds just exactly what it is: sometimes feeble and derivative in invention; sometimes commonplace material miraculously "lifted" by the charisma of a particular performer; but sometimes spell-bindingly original as when a witty phrase-maker such as Lorenz Hart is teamed with a musical genius such as Richard Rodgers (significantly there is more than one reference to Rogers and Hart songs in *A Dance to the Music of Time*). More and more do I find myself adhering to the attitude of the Viennese who, we are told, take their serious music lightly and their light music seriously.

One of the earliest 78s I bought was a 12" HMV of excerpts from Noël Coward's 1930 masterpiece *Private Lives*. The record label detailed the author himself in "dialogue with Gertrude Lawrence", a somewhat prosaic understatement for the extraordinary chemistry of their exchanges as the sparring couple on side A in the "Love Scene from Act 1". Just before Miss Lawrence, as Amanda, essays "Someday I'll Find You" in that wonderfully silvery voice which goes so endearingly off-key whenever she sustains a note, her ex-husband Elyot, from an adjacent hotel balcony in the South of France, comments on what a remarkably small repertoire the resident orchestra seems to have. She replies, "strange, how potent sheet music is". Or at least, that's what I always *thought* she said until I actually read the play and discovered that the line is, in fact, "strange, how potent *cheap* music is". *Pace* Coward, I've always preferred my original mis-hearing because, as a long-time collector of sheet music, it holds an additional truth for me. In any case, I never considered Coward's song "cheap". Curiously, most published editions of *Private Lives* give the line as *"extraordinary* how potent" but that's definitely not what Gertie says: presumably sanctioned by Noël, she uses the exact word Lord Byron did when he was similarly distracted by an off-stage band and nostalgically re-connected with the Past.

When I first read *A Dance to the Music of Time* in my mid-twenties, the musical references were naturally fascinating to me. Additionally, by that stage, the majority of them also meant something. Clearly the author was a man of some musical awareness. It wasn't until much later that I read Powell's memoirs where he claims to have "no musical sensitivities". But I'm sure he was underselling himself – he was obviously conversant with opera, for example, judging from the many references he makes to it in the novels. In any case, it's not all that unusual for connoisseurs of the Arts in general to have "blank spots" in particular areas. I remember at university my tutor in Italian, a perceptive literary scholar, clearly sensitive to words as well as to painting and sculpture, admitting that he simply didn't have any special taste for classical music and that it meant little to him. I was rather shocked at the time but I grew to realise that it's far from uncommon and not to be condemned. Many with a strong visual sense – Powell for example with his acute sensitivity to the Fine Arts – don't necessarily have a correspondingly strong aural one – or *vice versa*.

I would in any case be prepared to give Powell the benefit of the doubt if (as Kingsley Amis claimed) he nodded off after dinner while a recording of Constant Lambert's music was on the gramophone. It may simply have been the combined effects of a large meal, an overheated room and a decent brandy. In any case, given the abundance of musical references in *A Dance to the Music of Time*, Powell clearly wasn't at odds with St Cecilia and I'm sure she extends her patronage just as much to a catchy fox-trot as to a highbrow symphony. For a supposedly "non-musical" man, Powell throws in a huge variety of musical allusions, both classical and popular. This is why Jeff Manley's music guide to the novel sequence, most impressively researched, is a fascinating and inestimable companion. It gathers together a wealth of references, many of them identifiable but in danger of being forgotten; some tantalisingly allusive but now revealed in context; only a very few downright elusive – and that's probably Powell's own fault. In all cases this superb guide fills in the background in a way that I've found fascinating and from which I've learnt so much. I know it will prove invaluable in years to come when the music of Powell's era will be even more underplayed and undervalued than it is nowadays, a decade after his death. Jeff Manley has done a wonderful job in keeping these musical references alive and preserving their meaning. For if we cannot "hear" the tunes themselves and realise what song they are singing, then we can hardly hope to follow all the intricate steps of the *Dance* itself.

Paul Guinery
June 2010

Guide to the Musical References

Albert Hall
Concert hall in South Kensington, London, dedicated to the memory of Prince Albert by Queen Victoria and opened by her in 1871. It is officially named the Royal Albert Hall and has a maximum seating capacity of 8,000. [See BRAHMS and WAGNER (*CCR*, 4, 13, 23).] The Royal College of Music, where Moreland studied, is just behind the Albert Hall (*KO*, 83). Powell's first remembered boyhood home was at 25 Albert Hall Mansions, just next door to the Albert Hall (*Infants*, 41-47).

AMBROSE (1896/97-1971)
Stage name of Benjamin Baruch (or Bert) Ambrose, English bandleader and violinist, who was usually simply referred to as Ambrose. He was born in the East End of London but reached his first success as a professional musician in New York. He returned to London and in 1922 started an orchestra which first performed at The Embassy Club (*qv.*) where he stayed until 1927 (with a year or so in between back in New York). He then moved to The Mayfair Hotel, Stratton Street, London, where he was also able to broadcast live performances, and remained there until 1933. He is commemorated there by a Blue Plaque. Ambrose is noted for, *inter alia*, his discovery of English singer Dame Vera Lynn DBE (b. 1917) who sang with his orchestra between 1937-1940 and later earned the nickname "The Forces Sweetheart" in WWII.

Archie Gilbert mentions that Ambrose will be playing at one of the parties he will attend after the Walpole-Wilsons' dinner party, expecting that this party (given by a Mrs Samson) will be "better than the Huntercombes' ... though of course the band is not everything" (*BM*, 50). [See "*Arm in arm together*", *Popular Music from Lilliburlero to Lili Marlene* and *Balls, Picnics and Parties*.] [See also *WN*, 160.]

"*Angels in the height, adore him*"
Beginning of final verse of the hymn *Praise, My Soul, the King of Heaven*; original words by Henry F Lyte (1793-1847) were based on Psalm 103; music (*Lauda anima*) by John Goss (1800-80), first published in 1869. This hymn is sung at the Victory Thanksgiving Service in St Paul's as the Royal Party reach their seats. Jenkins notes that, as in the hymn, the congregation is "gathered in from every race" (*MP*, 221). The words of the hymn quoted by Jenkins are a variant of Lyte's original version. This variant was included in the *Hymns Ancient and Modern* collection first published in 1861 after Lyte's death, with changes by the editors to reflect their disapproval of the notions that angels would help mortals worship God and that the sun and moon would bow down before Him. [See *Penguin Book of Hymns* (London, 1989, Ian Bradley, editor).] The version as quoted by Jenkins and appearing in the

service sheet for the thanksgiving service prevailed for a time but more recent hymnals (*eg. The New English Hymnal*) have reverted to Lyte's original:

> *Angels, help us to adore Him:*
> *Ye behold Him face to face;*
> *Sun and moon bow down before Him,*
> *Dwellers all in time and space.*

"Après la guerre, there'll be a good time everywhere"
World War I song. Words and music by BC Hilliam (1890-1968), Canadian-born British composer, writer, lyricist and musical director. Published in 1917. The song was popularized in the post-war years by Elsie Janis (née Bierbower) (1889-1956), an American musical comedy star who was active in entertaining the British and American troops in WWI (including in the front lines), earning the sobriquet "the sweetheart of the AEF" (Allied Expeditionary Force). She sang the song in the London revue *Hullo America!* which opened at the Palace Theatre on 25 September 1918 and ran for 358 performances. She later sang the song again in the New York revue *Elsie Janis and Her Gang* which opened on 1 December 1919 and ran for over 3 years. The song is hummed by Jeavons "when in poor form". Jeavons' recitation reminds Jenkins of how different was the more optimistic mood following "the earlier conflict" from that following WWII (*BDFR* 2).

L'Après-midi d'un faune (The Afternoon of a Faun)
Ballet choreographed by Vaslav Nijinsky (*qv.*) and first performed in Paris by the Russian Ballet (*qv.*) in 1912. The music was Claude Debussy's (*qv.*) *Prélude à l'après-midi d'un faune*, composed for orchestra and first performed in 1894. Both the ballet and the music were inspired by Stéphane Mallarmé's poem *L'après-midi d'un faune* published in 1876. Nijinsky danced the lead part himself. His portrayal of the faun was, in the words of Lydia Sokolova, an English dancer in the company, "so animal that one expected him to run up the side of the hill with [the nymph's scarf] in his mouth ... There was an unforgettable moment ... when he knelt on one leg on top of the hill, with his other leg stretched out behind him".

Norman Chandler strikes a similar pose backstage, after his performance with Matilda in *The Duchess of Malfi*: "He put his head on one side, forefinger against cheek, transforming himself to some character of ballet, perhaps the Faun from *L'Après-midi*". Matilda applaudingly informs him of his Nijinsky-like qualities (*CCR*, 48-49).

"Arm in arm together"
Corporal Gwylt (*qv.*) is overheard by Jenkins and Captain Gwatkin singing this song to Maureen the barmaid in June 1940 (*VB*, 228-29). This leads to Gwatkin's discovery that Maureen has been unfaithful. [See also *WN*, 103

where "Welsh troops" are singing this song.] Jenkins describes the song as recalling old fashioned music-hall tunes of fifty years before but says that it was, in fact, contemporary to that moment and popular among the men. The song was written by Jim Church and Stan Bradbury and published in 1940. It was recorded by Ambrose and his Orchestra (*qv.*) in March of that same year with a vocal by Jack Cooper (Decca F7440).

"As o'er each continent and island"
Line from the hymn *The Day Thou Gavest, Lord, is Ended*. The words are by John Ellerton (1826-93) and the tune to which it is most usually sung – and which was composed for it – is *St Clement of Alexandria* by Clement Scholefield (1839-1904), who was for a time chaplain of Eton College.

The hymn is sung by the congregation in the school chapel immediately following Le Bas' arrest in the "Braddock alias Thorne" incident. Uncharacteristically, Stringham does not join in the singing despite the partiality to hymns he later expresses in the normal run of things. Widmerpool, on the other hand, is "singing hard: his mouth opening and shutting sharply, more than ever like some uncommon specimen of marine life". Jenkins wonders whether the same thought expressed in the quoted verse is passing through Widmerpool's mind as he sings, since the words of the verse seem "especially applicable" to Widmerpool, who was leaving school at the end of term. Jenkins himself

> *felt rather moved as the hymn rolled on. A group of boys behind me began to chant a descant of their own; making a good deal of noise, not entirely disagreeable.*

Widmerpool "stopped singing for a second and ... glanced across reprovingly". That is Jenkins' last memory of Widmerpool at school, as "he left, for good, a few weeks later" (*QU*, 50-51).

AUBER, Daniel Francois Esprit (1782-1871)
French composer. Identified by Bob Duport, when encountered by Jenkins in Brussels during the November 1944 European tour of the Military Attachés, as composer of the opera *La Muette de Portici* (*The Mute Woman of Portici*) first performed in Paris in 1828. Duport notes that this opera had been recently performed in Brussels to celebrate the liberation from the Germans. Duport also explains that this same opera, when it had its Brussels debut (in 1830), so excited the Belgians that "they kicked the Hollanders out". He also makes a pun on the title character of the opera when he says that, while not particularly keen on Auber, "I've met a lot of *dumb girls*, so I've been to hear it several times to remind myself of them" (italics supplied). The story of the opera is based on the 1647 popular uprising in Naples against Spanish rule led by the 25 year-old fisherman Masaniello, a leading character in the opera, and *Masaniello* is an alternative title.

The revelation of Duport's "musical leanings" demonstrates to Jenkins that "people can always produce something unexpected about themselves" (*MP*, 190). In this case the revelation should not have been totally unexpected since Jimmy Brent had told Jenkins, only a few years before, that Duport knew a good deal more than one would believe "about art and all that", causing Jenkins to muse that "there were important sides of [Duport] that I had missed" (*VB*, 124-25).

"Aut Sousa, aut nihil"
Reference to John Philip Sousa (1854-1932), American composer best known for his military marches such as *Stars and Stripes Forever*. Moreland replaces "Caesar" with "Sousa" in the Latin quote usually taken to mean "all or nothing". This quotation is offered by Moreland in response to Audrey Maclintick's anecdote regarding matrimonial troubles experienced by a friend whose first husband used to come home at 4 AM and play military marches on the gramophone (*CCR*, 174). [See also *WN*, 6.]

Ave Maria
Musical setting (1859) by Charles Gounod (*qv.*) of the prayer to the Virgin Mary. Gounod wrote the music over the Prelude No.1 in C-Major of Johann Sebastian Bach's *The Well-Tempered Clavier, Book I* (1722) (which was also used by British rock group Procol Harum in their 1967 hit *A Whiter Shade of Pale*). General Conyers is overheard playing this piece on the 'cello when Jenkins arrives at his Sloane Square flat for a visit, and later the General notes that he hasn't quite mastered the passage "*Nunc et in hora mortis nostrae*". He then hums through the remainder of the piece, while conducting "through the air the strokes of an imaginary baton" (*LM*, 69-72); still later he sits in silence, pondering matters involving Widmerpool and his sister-in-law Mildred Haycock "or, more probably, his own rendering of Gounod" (*LM*, 78); and at the end of Jenkins' visit the General is "occasionally murmuring faint musical intonations that might be ringing the changes on *nunc et in hora*" (*LM*, 86).

The Bag of Nails
Night club to which Stringham proposes to take Audrey Maclintick as a means of escape from his mother's reception following the debut of Moreland's symphony. This club was offered as an alternative to that of Dickie Umfraville's in the event that the latter had closed (*CCR*, 182, 184). The Bag o' Nails was, in the 1930s, a venue located in the basement of a building on Kingly Street, Soho, quite near to Mrs Foxe's party at her home in Berkeley Square. At the time Stringham made his proposal to Audrey, the Bag was a noted showplace for the dance bands of the day, although he was probably more interested in the flexible drinking hours for which it was also well known. In the words of a contemporary journalist,

> *It is to the history of British swing music what Hampton Court*
> *Palace is to the history of England. It is the show shop of*
> *promising musicians; the rendezvous of successful ones.*

[See *Anthony Powell Society Newsletter*, **40**, 9-11; also article by David Butler in *Anthony Powell Society Newsletter*, **28**, 12-13.]

In the 1960s it had a revival as a venue for noted rock performers and is most closely associated with Jimi Hendrix who made an early UK appearance there in 1966. Paul McCartney of The Beatles is said to have met his first wife, Linda Eastman, in this club during a 1967 performance by Georgie Fame and the Blue Flames. The Bag is, as this is written (Summer 2010), undergoing another attempted revival at 9 Kingly Street, and its webpage (*http://www.bagonailssoho.co.uk*) cites references in Powell's novel as a selling point.

BAKST, Léon (1866-1924)

A portrait of King Victor Emmanuel II (1820-78, reigned as King of Italy 1861-78) hanging in Foppa's club reminds Jenkins of the costume designs of Bakst for one of the early Russian ballets (*AW*, 145). He is referring to Léon Bakst, Russian painter and costume / scene designer, who made a name for himself as a stage designer in Paris with the Russian Ballet (*qv.*) beginning in 1908. In his memoirs, Powell also recalls reading, as a child, a book of his father's with reproductions of Bakst's designs for the Russian Ballet, "the Chief Eunuch in *Schéhérazade* seeming to me a picture of incredible beauty" (*Infants*, 48). His art, according to Powell, expressed "implications of irony, disillusionment, cruelty that add force to ... Russian Ballet design" (*Infants*, 88).

"Balls, Picnics and Parties, – Picnics, Parties and Balls"

Popular song "chanted at the top of her voice" by Heather Hopkins after she leaves the Chelsea flat of Eleanor Walpole-Wilson and Norah Tolland with the egg she has just borrowed (*LM*, 96). The music was written by George Christie with words by Charley Fredericks and was published in 1927. The refrain, which Heather is singing, goes as follows:

> *Balls, picnics and parties – Picnics, parties and balls –*
> *Some people like to go out to a show,*
> *Others stay home with an old radio,*
> *(But) Balls, picnics and parties – Are mem'ries I love to recall –*
> *You can have nightclubs and swell cabarets,*
> *The sports that I love have them beat forty ways.*
> *Balls, picnics and parties – Picnics, parties and balls.*

A recording of a song by this title was made in 1932 or 1933 by the White Star Syncopators which included a vocal solo by British dance band singer

Sam Browne (1898-1972). That recording (Piccadilly 900) would probably still have been in circulation at the time Heather sings the song in 1934. Browne was active as a recording artist throughout the 1930's with several bands and is particularly remembered for singing with Ambrose and his Orchestra (*qv.*) at The Mayfair Hotel and The Embassy Club. One source on dance music recordings of the 1930s suggests that the band which backed Browne's vocal was possibly made up of members of the Ambrose Orchestra put together for purposes of this recording.

"Baron Scarpia"
Villain (a baritone) in the opera *Tosca* (1900) by Italian composer Giacomo Puccini (1858-1924). He is Chief of Police of Rome who is slain by Tosca to liberate her lover, Cavaradossi, from his clutches. Maclintick refers to Buster Foxe as Baron Scarpia after Jenkins requests Irish whiskey from him on Maclintick's behalf, apparently likening Buster's powers over the whiskey to those of Scarpia over Tosca and her lover. As it turns out, Buster's cellar contains no Irish whiskey (*CCR,* 148).

The Bartered Bride
Opera by Bedřich Smetana (*qv.*), Czech composer, first performed in its definitive three act version in 1870. Offered as one of Colonel Hlava's "musical occasions" mounted by the Czechoslovak civil authorities for one of their "national causes". Colonel Hlava explains that the heroine is not a bride but a fiancée and is not bartered but sold (*Die Verkaufte Braut* in German, a literal translation of the Czech title *Prodaná nevěsta*). The convoluted plot involves a projected marriage between the heroine, Mařenka, on the one hand, and either her sweetheart Jeník or the simpleton Vašek, on the other. This is all explained in the „country fair' scene in Act 1. A payment is made to Jeník by a marriage-broker, seeming to induce his acceptance of Mařenka's arranged marriage to Vašek. In the Act 3 denouement, however, the plot bestows upon Mařenka the right to choose between the two and she chooses Jeník, just as the hapless Vašek appears in the form of the "man disguised as a bear", having agreed to replace the drunken circus performer originally scheduled to play that role.

Prince Theodoric is in attendance with the Huntercombes, Lord Huntercombe being listed in the programme as serving on the board that sponsored the performance. Pamela Flitton arrives late, accompanied by Lady McReith, and is noticed by Widmerpool, also in attendance, who recalls having seen her previously with some Americans at "one of Biddle's big Allied gatherings", probably referring to Anthony Joseph Drexel Biddle Jr (1896-1961), Philadelphia socialite who achieved the rank of Major General and later US Ambassador to various allied countries in London exile during WWII, including Czechoslovakia. It is at this performance that Pamela makes a public show of affection for Theodoric but is politely rebuffed (*MP*, 96-102). [See also MONTEZ, Lola.]

BEETHOVEN, Ludwig van (1770-1827)

German composer and pianist. Moreland is described by Jenkins as having been "physically formed in a ,musical' mould ... with a massive, Beethoven-shaped head" (*CCR*, 16).

BENNETT, Billy (1887-1942)

Stage name of William Robertson Russell Bennett DCM MM, British music hall comedian who was billed as "almost a gentleman", which is the title applied to a collection of his routines still in circulation. In a 1945 book review of a survey of light entertainment on the London stage in the 1920s-30s, Powell described him as one of the "giant figures" of that period. [See Anthony Powell, "Song and Dance", *The New English Review*, July 1945, 280.] He is credited by Jeavons as the source of the song sung by the latter upon hearing that Hugo Tolland had enlisted in the Army (*KO*, 239):

> *I'm a trooper, I'm a trooper,*
> *And my name is Gladys Cooper.*

While Jeavons (or Powell) may well have heard Bennett perform this number, it does not seem to have survived into his published works. Gladys Cooper is, however, mentioned in at least one of Bennett's surviving monologues, *My Mother Doesn't Know I'm On the Stage:*

> *The day she met me out with Gladys Cooper*
> *She started screaming, "Murder" and "Police!"*

Dame Gladys Constance Cooper DBE (1888-1971) was a British stage, film and television actress who achieved a considerable success over a period extending back to 1909 and was still active up to the time of her death. Besides being female and possessing a name rhyming with "trooper", her appearance in Bennett's song takes on added humour from her career as an actress whose reputation was made playing rather snooty roles in which she would have looked down her nose at the likes of Bennett and Jeavons.

BERLIOZ, Hector (1803-69)

French Romantic composer who is best known for his *Symphonie Fantastique* (1830). Emily Brightman, in describing the Romanticism lurking under Russell Gwinnett's "staid exterior", compares him to Berlioz (and Byron) (*TK*, 50). Berlioz also wrote *Damnation of Faust* (*La damnation de Faust*), called a *légende dramatique*, which was a work for orchestra, voices and chorus, with a libretto he adapted from Goethe's *Faust*. It was first performed in 1846.

Moreland says he had read that "Spanish fleas have their own national song – a three-four tune in F major that Berlioz introduces into the *Damnation of Faust*". His source for this is a life of Chabrier (*qv.*) in which that composer provides the information about the Spanish fleas (*CCR,* 119). Moreland (and Chabrier) here refer to Part Two, Scene 6, of *The Damnation of Faust* in which Mephistopheles takes Faust into a tavern where another character takes up "The Song of the Rat", followed by a mocking *"Requiescat in Pace"* for the dead rat and a comic fugue on the word "Amen". Mephistopheles then counters with "The Song of the Flea", which consists of a twitchy, skipping accompaniment imitating the insect. Both songs also appear in Goethe's *Faust, Part 1: Auerbach's Cellar in Leipzig* and the words of the Berlioz version are based on Goethe's text.

The Best Things in Life Are Free
Moreland may be referring to the popular tune when he opines that despite

> *never myself having been more than one of a pair [in a sexual encounter]* ... **the best things in life are free.**
> (Emphasis supplied) (*TK*, 90) [See also *WN*, 45]

The song was written by a three-man team of US songwriters Lew Brown (1893-1958) (who also wrote the lyrics for *Dapper Dan* (*qv.*)), Buddy de Sylva (1895-1950) and Ray Henderson (1896-1970). It was first performed in the Broadway musical *Good News* (1927), with film versions of that play in 1930 and 1947; the song itself became the title of a Hollywood movie about the songwriters released in 1956.

The Bing Boys
One of the most popular musical revues in London during World War I. Jeavons mentions it to Jenkins as representing something from a different way of life that prevailed before the war (*LM,* 177-78). He is referring to the revue that opened at the Alhambra Theatre in Leicester Square in April 1916 – *The Bing Boys Are Here*. It was written by George Grossmith Jr (1879-1935, son of George Grossmith who, with his brother Weedon, wrote the novel *Diary of a Nobody,* published in 1892 and still in print) and Fred Thompson. The play continued as *The Bing Girls Are There,* which opened in February 1917, and as *The Bing Boys on Broadway,* which opened in February 1918, with some of the original cast returning but with different songs and story. All told, the three versions ran for over 1000 performances. Jeavons remarks that Jenkins was probably too young to have seen *The Bing Boys,* but Jenkins says that he had managed to see it as a schoolboy. Which version each of them saw is not indicated. [See also *If You Were the Only Girl in the World*.]

Bithel's Dance **
On Bithel's arrival at the base in South Wales, his fellow officers plant a
dummy in his bed as a "new boy" rag. The dummy has his boots as feet and
his sponge bag as a head, adorned with his "fore-and-aft" khaki cap. Bithel
arrives inebriated in his bedroom, but, when he sees the dummy, begins an
impromptu dance in an apparent effort to get even with the raggers. This
begins with his hands above his head, "tripping slowly round the bed ... as if
following the known steps of a ritual dance". He even sings to the dummy,
intoning "A song of love ... A song of love". The dance becomes
"increasingly grotesque [with Bithel] undulating his arms in oriental fashion".
Toward the end, he "violently rocked his body from side to side in a religious
ecstasy ... kicking out his feet in a country measure". At the same time he
chants endearments to the dummy, ending with "Love 'o mine ... Love 'o
mine", after he collapses on the bed himself. By that time, the raggers have
left the room, leaving only Jenkins as a witness. Jenkins concludes that by
doing the dance "Bithel has shown himself equal to being ragged [and] come
out completely on top of those who had tried to make him look silly" (*VB*, 24-
29, 174).

BRAHMS, Johannes (1833-97)
German composer intensely disliked by Moreland. He warns Mr Deacon not
to go near the Albert Hall because of the risk that he might be forced to listen
to the music of Brahms (or, worse yet, be tempted to do so of his own free
will) (*CCR*, 13). Mr Deacon responds that he has heard enough of
Moreland's "youthful prejudices", in particular his "sentiments regarding the
orchestration of the Second Piano Concerto" (*qv.*).

During the war, Moreland expresses the willingness to be "like Brahms and
play the piano in a brothel – even play Brahms' own compositions in a
brothel, part of the *Requiem* would be very suitable" if only he could leave
London and the blackout behind, even if it meant going to "somewhere like
Saigon or Bangkok" (*SA*, 134). It has long been believed that in his youth
Brahms supplemented his family's income by playing in bars that also housed
brothels in his hometown of Hamburg. Although challenged, these stories
seem to have originated with Brahms himself. As to Moreland's longing to
translate himself to Saigon, it was a desire he shared with Constant Lambert,
according to Powell's memoirs (*Strangers*, 141).

Bugle Calls
Two bugle calls mentioned in a discussion involving Jenkins, Gwatkin,
Kedward and Cadwallader are referred to as *Alarm* and *Cookhouse* (*VB*, 177-
78). These are among the list of routine bugle calls for the British Army
(Infantry and Mounted Infantry) but are more formally called *Alarm (for
troops to turn out under arms*) and *Men's Meal (1ˢᵗ Call)*, respectively. The
words associated with these calls by Gwatkin and Cadwallader are, as

Gwatkin indicates, a matter of "military lore" and seem to have no official status. But given the multiplicity of bugle calls (the routine list for Infantry and Mounted Infantry includes over 40 calls), the easily remembered words must have helped the soldiers more quickly identify each call.

In the novel, General Liddament decides to use *Alarm* to warn the troops of any local uprising among the Irish. To make sure the call would be understood, "all ranks were paraded to hear the *Alarm* sounded". Those insufficiently musical to understand it have to rely on the unofficial words, which CSM Cadwallader only reluctantly reveals are: "*Sergeant-Major's-got-a-horn!*" (*VB*, 178-79). *Alarm* is also the bugle call sounded by actor Sam Jaffe, in what may be the most well-known fictional application of British Army bugle calls, playing the role of Gunga Din at the dramatic climax of the film of that title released in early 1939, about a year before Cadwallader is required to repeat the words.

Jenkins recalls, as a child, hearing a bugle call "shrill, yet desperately sad", identified for him as *Defaulters* by Private Bracey on their way to see an inter-regimental football match (*KO,* 26). This is still on the list of routine calls and is used to summon those otherwise confined to barracks for disciplinary purposes relating to minor infringements of the rules such as having a dirty kit, being late for parade *etc.* There is an example of a "defaulter" at Castlemallock who is being pressed rather vociferously by a sergeant to perform the punitive tasks imposed upon him (*VB,* 173-74). Defaulters were regularly summoned to inspection at the guardroom where they were also often assigned more duties. At least one version of the unofficial words is "You can be a defaulter as long as you like | As long as you answer your name", while another concludes "as long as you answer the call", and they both fit the tune for this call used by the British Army (Infantry and Mounted Infantry). The trip to an inter-regimental football match (it is not clear if this is rugby or soccer) accompanied by his father's soldier-servant is recorded in Powell's memoirs, but not the bugle call (*Infants,* 54). Dicky Umfraville also claims to have heard *Defaulters* called after a bad day at the races (*TK,* 3). [See "*Trumpeter, what call are you sounding now?*"]

Café de Madrid **
Night club venue where Heather Hopkins and Max Pilgrim are booked to perform in 1934, about a month after Heather looked in on Norah Tolland and Eleanor Walpole-Wilson to borrow an egg (*LM,* 95). Their act is a flop at the Madrid; according to Peter Templer, this is because it was too old-fashioned. The act is demoted to Dicky Umfraville's new club where Peter and the others hear it later that year (*LM,* 190). Max had had at least one earlier chance at the Madrid during Matilda Wilson's run in the *Duchess of Malfi*; this would have been about 1933 (*CCR,* 48, 51).

During the war, Max is engaged in entertaining the troops under the auspices of ENSA (*qv.*) but is released from that arrangement, according to Moreland, "to do a brief season at the Madrid as a kind of rest". This would be in early 1941 and would consist of "a revival there of some of his old songs – *Tess of Le Touquet; Heather, Heather, she's under the weather*, all those", according to Chips Lovell, who was shortly to leave for the Madrid from the nearby Café Royal where he was having dinner with Jenkins (*SA,* 115-16). At the time of the Madrid engagement, Max is a lodger of Moreland and Audrey Maclintick and, after his act at the Madrid, Max was expected to join them at the Café Royal, where they were also dining with Jenkins,. When Max fails to appear at the Café Royal, Audrey wonders what's happened to him. "That turn must be over. It's a short one anyway, and he comes on early at the Madrid". Odo Stevens and Priscilla Lovell then join the party at the Café Royal. Odo has also read about Max's revival and wants to visit the Madrid but is dissuaded by Priscilla (who is probably motivated as much by her wishing to avoid a meeting of Odo and Chips as by her alleged dislike of Max's music) (*SA,* 145). While Max's songs were beginning to date even in the 1920's, now that the war had given rise to a demand for "all that was most nostalgic" he was again in demand (*SA,* 153-54). If Audrey was correct, however, Max's revival act at the Madrid was, apparently, a warm-up, not the main event.

Max is performing the night the Madrid was destroyed by a bomb that fell during the middle of his act: "It was getting the bird in a big way. Never experienced the like before, even on a tour". Bijou Ardglass was celebrating her fortieth birthday at the Madrid that same night, and Chips Lovell attended the party. Max was only slightly injured and responds to Jenkins' questions about the others: "I'm afraid it was Bijou's last party ... Bijou's table was where [the bomb] came through the ceiling ... No one survived from that corner", including Chips Lovell (*SA,* 155-57). That same night Lady Molly and Priscilla (who goes home rather than joining Chips at the Madrid) are killed when a bomb hit the rear of Lady Molly's flat in South Kensington. When these events are recounted later to Stringham, he recalls a night at the Madrid in the early days of his marriage to Peggy Stepney: "The evening was a total frost" (*SA,* 222).

The Café de Madrid is the fictional name for the Café de Paris, a night club of similar description which suffered a bomb attack on 8 March 1941, very much like the one Max describes. In real life, the band leader who was onstage at the time of the attack – Ken "Snakehips" Johnson (stage name of Kenrick Reginald Hymans Johnson (1914-1941) Guyana-born, British bandleader) – was one of those killed. The Café de Paris was rebuilt after the war and, as of this writing, still functions as a venue for music and other forms of entertainment at 3-4 Coventry Street W1 (north side between Piccadilly Circus and Leicester Square).

CAROLO **

Violinist. Real name Wilson or Wilkinson or Parker and first husband of Matilda Wilson (née Betty Updike) who later married Hugh Moreland and, later still, Sir Magnus Donners. His

> *face was pale and drawn, his black hair arranged in delicate waves, this consciously „romantic' appearance and demeanour altogether misrepresenting his character, which was ... far from imaginative.*

Spent years as a child prodigy. Moreland heard an early performance at the Wigmore Hall (*qv.*) (*CCR,* 20). According to Maclintick, "played Sarasate (*qv.*) up and down the country clad as Little Lord Fauntleroy" (*CCR,* 25). Plays Second Violin at the *Seraglio* benefit concert, where his "romantic raven locks, now snow white, had been allowed to grow comparatively long, in the manner of Liszt, to whom Carolo bore some slight resemblance"; lacks the warmth of the old Venetian street singer when taking his bows after the performance (*TK,* 238-40).

CASANOVA, Giacomo (1725-98)

Among his attributes (if that's the right word), Casanova is said by Moreland to be something of a musician.

> *In early life, Casanova played the violin – like Carolo. Casanova played in a band. I doubt if he would have been up to a solo performance ... Besides, he much fancied himself as a figure at the opera and musical parties. (CCR, 32)*

Moreland's recollection is consistent with Casanova's life story, according to which at about the age of 20 he was a violinist in the San Samuele theatre in Venice. In his memoirs, Powell says that "Casanova may also have collaborated in writing the libretto of Mozart's *Don Giovanni*" (*Strangers,* 88). [See also SPURLING, Book Index, *"How Happy I could be with either"*, *Don Juan* and LORTZING.]

CHABRIER, (Alexis) Emmanuel (1841-94)

French composer whose mention in *CCR* is one of the most pivotal musical references in *Dance.* Chabrier was born in the Auvergne (well to the east of where Jenkins stays with the Leroys in Touraine) and attended school in Clermont-Ferrand. He moved to Paris with his family at the age of fifteen, and his musical talent quickly emerged. Despite his tremendous promise as a pianist, though, his family insisted that he go to law school. He did so, and, with these credentials, embarked on a career as what Powell would style, in the French manner, an *haute functionnaire* – a powerful civil servant, though hopefully a more constructive one than Blackhead. During these years, his musical emphasis switched from performing to composing. He wrote operettas, piano pieces, and began to conceive larger symbolic and operatic works. Chabrier was friendly with many writers, some of whom worked on librettos for his operettas and operas; one of his most prominent friends was the poet Paul Verlaine. A visit to Munich in 1880, where he heard a performance of Wagner's *Tristan*, was a cathartic moment for Chabrier, who began work on a large, Wagnerian opera, *Gwendoline*. Support for the project in the Paris musical world was, however, fitful, and its premiere in 1886, at Brussels' Theatre de la Monnaie, was anticlimactic. Chabrier's subsequent operatic work, *Briseis* (1888), was sagely dubbed a *drame lyrique* to forestall Wagnerian comparisons. Chabrier's admiration of Wagner (*qv.*), combined with his perceived inability to reproduce a Wagnerian largeness of scale, is often seen as evidence that the Gallic musical temperament, with its undergirding by a sense of rationality and precision, could not reproduce the ambitious scale of Wagner's musical totality.

Chabrier's quintessentially Gallic sensibility, indeed, did not prevent him from reaching out to other European countries for musical precedents and inspiration. It is such an international journey of his that crops up in *Dance*. His symphonic work (formally called a rhapsody), *España* (1883), is the only large scale work of Chabrier's to receive unhesitating critical acclaim. It is this work that is alluded to when Moreland, reading a biography of Chabrier that Maclintick has in his house, says "I've been looking at this book on Chabrier ... what an enjoyable time he had in Spain" (Chabrier, in his letters from Spain during his "research" for the work, wrote explicitly erotic meditations on the beauty of Spanish women, which may well have been the particular object of Moreland's diagnosis of pleasure) (*CCR*, 110). The implication of Chabrier's mention in *Dance* is twofold. It reflects the omnipresence of Spain (the Spanish Civil War) as a *leitmotif* in *CCR*, and links the urgency of Spain as an issue across the political spectrum in the 1930s to earlier nineteenth-century *espagnolerie*. [See also *Iberia*.]

The Chabrier mention also serves as a bridge between the musical and political worlds of *CCR*. Although Chabrier is often described as a Romantic composer, and certainly is so in theme and temperament, there is also a playful, cerebral quality, evidenced no more than in the perceived failure of most of his "major", more emotionally expansive works that suits the aesthetic espoused by Moreland and, inferentially, Powell. Chabrier's music is at once more intellectual *and* more erotic than that of most of his contemporaries. While distrusting a pure or unfettered romanticism, Moreland, in life and art, has powerful romantic yearnings, laced by a sharp, ironic self-awareness. Chabrier serves as a shorthand for these interweaving tendencies. Also, like Moreland, Chabrier came to a relatively early and tragic end, dying prematurely of syphilis (coincidently, Chabrier's life span is almost identical with that of Moreland.)

Strikingly, even though Maclintick owns the biography of Chabrier, Maclintick is so dour and is immersed in his own personal melancholy to such an extent that he does not wish to discuss Chabrier. There does not, incidentally, appear to have been an "actual" biography of Chabrier in English before Rollo Myers' of 1969, but Moreland could certainly have been able to read French proficiently enough to enjoy René Martineau's 1910 French biography. The 1928 revival of Chabrier's 1887 operetta *Le Roi Malgré Lui* could arguably have contributed to his popularity in the era of *CCR* (*CCR*, 109, 110, 115, 119). [See also BERLIOZ.]

CHALIAPIN, Feodor Ivanovich (1873-1938)

Russian opera singer (a bass) of the first half of the 20th century. Considered one of the greatest performers in the history of opera, he is credited with promoting the tradition of naturalistic acting in opera. After performing in Russia, Italy and the US, he was introduced to London and Paris by Serge Diaghilev (*qv.*) in 1913. At that point he began to offer solo performances that included Russian folk songs, such as *The Song of the Volga Boatmen* (*qv.*), which he made famous throughout the world. He also appeared in GW Pabst's *Don Quixote* in 1933, around the time of the setting of *AW*.

Jean Duport, during her affair with Jenkins, relates to him the details of a dinner given by her brother Peter at the Carlton Grill, making rather a point of how boring two businessmen in the party had been. In an effort to flatter Jenkins by assuming he had a knowledge of music superior to that of Peter's friends, she specifically notes that one of them had "never heard of Chaliapin". Jimmy Brent turns out to have been one of these two businessmen, but his identity is concealed by Jean. Brent later recounts to Jenkins his version of the Carlton Grill evening when they meet each other on a military training course at Aldershot. Jenkins proposes to himself to determine whether Brent is the musical ignoramus to whom Jean had referred, by singing "*The Song of the Volga Boatmen*" if necessary, to prove the point that Brent lacks any experience of opera. His examination of Brent is, however, pre-empted by Brent's revelation that he had had an affair with Jean (a fact which Jenkins already knows from Duport) that began the day after the Carlton Grill dinner when Jean telephoned him (of which both Jenkins and Duport were unaware). Nor were either of them aware that it was Brent, not Jean, who broke off their affair (*VB*, 128-33).

Furthering the mystery, the Chaliapin point brings up an intriguing crux. Jean's derision of Brent seems to suggest that she, Jean, does claim musical knowledge. Yet Bob Duport, when speaking of his wife, says: "... she only knew *God Save the King* because everybody stood up" (*MP*, 190). How could Jean then know about Chaliapin?

Aside from authorial inconsistency, which is always the least interesting solution of this kind of crux, several possibilities propose themselves. Firstly, Bob Duport could have been just insulting his former wife. Alternatively, Jean could have kept her musical side hidden from Bob just as she did her affair with Jenkins. Finally, Jean could have been as ignorant as Brent and issued a scrap of momentarily acquired musical knowledge to (a) flatter Jenkins that he was a classier sort of man than the philistines she met in other circumstances, or (b) throw him off the trail of Brent as an amorous rival. Interestingly, she focuses on her earlier affair with Jimmy Stripling, insisting that Jenkins acknowledge and come to terms with it, whereas the affair with Brent is concealed, perhaps because she has already decided at that moment to initiate it, or perhaps because Brent lacks the cultural panache possessed even by the race-car-driving, mysticism-pursuing Stripling.

The moment when Jean denounces Brent's philistinism is the point in her relationship with Nick where there seems the most intellectual and philosophical, as opposed to simply erotic, connection between them. That Jean is also being deceptive while saying this illustrates some of the reasons why their relationship went south – literally, as Jean leaves Nick to go with Bob to South America.

CHANDLER, Norman **
Actor and dancer, who is "rather a hand at the saxophone" (*CCR,* 22). Shares Moreland's love of mechanical pianos (*CCR,* 40). He functions as a host at Mrs Foxe's party for Moreland (*CCR,* 142-44, 147-48). In the later stages of his career, he becomes a theatrical director (*TK,* 226; *HSH,* 59). [See also *L'après-midi d'une faune* and *Die Entführung aus dem Serail.*] His career seems to be modelled in part on those of Powell's friends William Chappell (1907-1994) and Sir Frederick Ashton OM, CH, CBE (1904-1988) who both began as dancers at the Ballet Rambert and Vic-Wells Ballet during Constant Lambert's tenure as music director of the latter and who each later became a theatrical director and, respectively, a stage designer (Chappell) or a choreographer (Ashton).

Charleston
A dance step named for the city of Charleston, South Carolina. The dance was developed among African-American communities in the US but became popular internationally in the 1920's. In 1923, a dance tune called *The Charleston* was popularized by African-American composer / pianist James P Johnson (1894-1955) and appeared in the Broadway show *Runnin' Wild.* It became one of the most popular hits of the 1920's. In the novels, an elderly person in a dinner jacket is practising the Charleston near the Hyde Park Corner coffee stall as the group of partygoers gathers together before proceeding to Mrs Andriadis' house. Mr Deacon glances at the elderly dancer "with disapproval" (*BM,* 90). A similar dancer appears briefly in this same

scene of the Channel 4 TV film doing what appears to be an approximation of the Charleston.

CHOIRMASTER **

As recounted by Canon Fenneau, when Scorpio (then Leslie) Murtlock won a scholarship to a choir school (based at least to some extent on his success as a choirboy in Fenneau's parish church), "he developed a most unhappy influence over the choirmaster. Influence is a weak word in the circumstances". Fenneau is himself convinced, based on his personal acquaintance with both Murtlock and the choirmaster, that no "improper conduct" took place on the choirmaster's part – "not even pawing". The story ended tragically when the choirmaster, "his will ... altogether gone" sought transfer to another school where, although thought to be doing well, he drowned himself in the swimming pool "before the opening of the summer term" (*HSH,* 131-33).

Mr Cochran's Young Ladies

Refers to English impresario Charles Blake Cochran (1872-1951) – usually referred to as "CB" or "Cockie". In his memoirs Powell says that Cochran's stage productions "were renowned for their lavish settings and the good looks of the cast". In a discussion with Moreland, Jenkins dismisses the idea that Moreland was contemplating marriage with "one of Mr Cochran's Young Ladies". Barnby had put it about that Moreland pawned a cigarette case given him by Magnus Donners to entertain this *inamorata* at the Savoy, only to have her plead a headache as well as the curse, requiring the expenditure of most of the money to secure her return to Golders Green in a taxi (*CCR,* 7).

Another of Cochran's associates is also mentioned by Powell in his memoirs. She is described as a beautiful and intelligent woman enigmatically known as "Varda" (née Dorothy Farrer Stewart) (1901-51). She was born in New York City and may have met her first husband Jean "Janko" Varda (1893-1971) when they both appeared in a December 1919 *avant garde* production by the Art Theatre at the Haymarket in London: he in a "philosophical" ballet with dancer (and later ballet company director) Dame Marie Rambert (1888-1982) and she both in the ballet and in an ancient miracle play written by a 10th Century nun (opposite Basil Rathbone (1892-1967) who later became famous in films as Sherlock Holmes). Dorothy and Janko were married in 1921. She later appeared in a walk-on part in one of Cochran's shows at the London Pavilion after she had been somewhat summarily dropped by her first husband, who by that time was making a name for himself as a surrealist artist. She failed to capitalize on her stage appearances, however, and was afterwards set up in a bookshop by Michel Salaman ("a rich foxhunting art-loving friend of Augustus John"). The shop came into being about 1926, according to Powell, and was located on High Holborn where it "curves into Shaftesbury Avenue". Constant Lambert and Peter Quennell were each tenants in the two small flats above the bookshop. Lambert and others had to stand in as shop assistants from time to time when Varda had something better to do. On one such occasion when a female understudy (later identified as Phil Christov, née Crocker) was in charge, a customer asked whether the shop had a copy of Shelley's *Prometheus Unbound*. According to Powell, "the works of the Romantic School ... then not much in fashion, the proxy replied: „No, but I'm sure I've seen a bound copy on the shelves'."

Dorothy Varda was the model for Mrs Mendoza in Powell's pre-war novel *Agents and Patients* in which the book store was transformed into a flower shop. She was later married for a time to Powell's friend Gerald "The Squire" Reitlinger (1900-78) and later still to an official of the Treasury, Dennis Proctor. She took her own life in a cottage near Saffron Walden in 1951 (*Infants*, 95-97; *J87-89*, 33, 121).

COLLINS, José (1887-1958)
Stage name of Josephine Charlotte Collins. She was born into a theatrical family; her mother, Lottie Collins, made her name as a music hall performer whose signature turn was her rendition of the popular song *Ta-ra-ra-boom-de-ay*. Ted Jeavons feels some affinity for José because she, like him, married into the aristocracy (*LM,* 176). She was, for a time, Lady Robert Innes-Ker when she was married to Lord Robert Edward "Robin" Innes-Ker (1885-1958), youngest brother of Henry John Innes-Ker, the 8th Duke of Roxburghe (1876-1932). He first saw her in 1917 during WWI when, as a wounded guards officer, he attended a performance of *The Maid of the Mountains* (*qv.*) in which she played the lead and married her three years later in 1920, after what she describes as fairly persistent courtship and against the wishes of his mother, the Duchess of Roxburghe (1854-1923, who was born Lady Emily Spencer-Churchill, daughter of the 7th Duke of Marlborough). They were divorced in 1935.

Crystal Palace
Popular name for the glass-walled exhibition hall erected in Hyde Park in 1851 on the occasion of the Great Exhibition of the Works of Industry of All Nations, effectively the first "World's Fair". It was designed by Joseph Paxton (1803-65) who began his career as head gardener at the Chatsworth Estate in Derbyshire. After the exhibition closed, the structure was moved to Sydenham, South London, where it reopened in 1854. In 1857 a concert hall with an organ and seating for up to 4,000 was installed in the transept of the structure. Moreland's uncle saw Liszt (*qv.*) in this venue (*CCR,* 4). By the turn of the century, the building had deteriorated and in 1909 the owners went into receivership. Its fate was sealed in 1936 when it was destroyed in a fire. [See LISZT.]

Daly's Theatre

The musical play *The Maid of the Mountains* (*qv.*) and the song *Molly the Marchioness* (*qv.*) from the earlier musical play *The Country Girl* were both performed in this venue. Now demolished, it stood in the north-east corner of Leicester Square from 1893 to 1937. Ted Jeavons mentions seeing the former play performed there (*LM*, 175).

Damnation of Faust

See BERLIOZ.

"Dance of the Seven Veils"

Refers to the dance by Salomé, niece and step-daughter of King Herod, in the play of that name by Anglo-Irish poet and playwright Oscar Wilde (1854-1900) and the opera, based on that play, by Richard Strauss (*qv.*). Both works are based on the Biblical tale of King Herod and John the Baptist. In the theatrical / operatic version, Herod offers Salomé a gift of her choice if she will perform an unnamed dance, and, at the end of her dance, she asks for the head of John the Baptist on a platter. Although Herod is reluctant to grant the wish, Salomé is strongly supported by her mother Herodias, who is also Herod's wife. Having removed the veils at the dance's conclusion, she is supposed (at least in Wilde's stage directions) to throw herself naked at the feet of Herod, although that bit is often fudged. [But see Ida RUBINSTEIN.] The removal of the veils is analogized to Mrs Conyers extricating herself from a pile of wraps in the General's new motorcar when they arrive at Stonehurst (*KO*, 50). [See also *WN*, 98.]

"Dapper Dan was a very handy man"

Line from the song *Dapper Dan*, words by Lew Brown (1893-1958) and music by Albert von Tilzer (1878-1956), both Americans, published in 1921. The latter also wrote the music for the perennially popular American baseball classic "*Take Me Out to the Ball Game*" in 1908, while the former was part of a three-man songwriting team that wrote such hits as "*The Best Things In Life Are Free*" (*qv.*). The song is about a Pullman car porter and the line quoted is from the third verse:

> *Dapper Dan was a very handy man*
> *On a train that ran through Dixie.*
> *Made the beds and everything*
> *All you had to do was ring.*
> *If the train stopped anywhere,*
> *There'd be some gal waiting there.*
> *He'd say, "this is one of mine.*
> *And there's others down the line".*

A UK recording was made in November 1921 by British vocalist Jack Buchanan (1891-1957), who also performed the song in the 1921 West End revue *A to Z* produced by André Charlot (who also produced *Buzz-Buzz*) at the Prince of Wales Theatre in the Strand. Stringham recites the first line in December 1921 when Templer returns from London after a day off from school, describing him as "dressed as if you were going to dance up and down in front of a row of naked ladies singing [this song] or something equally lyrical" (*QU,* 30).

"Dearest, our day is over"
Moreland gently intones this turn-of-the-century popular song as he wards off an "acute attack of nostalgia" prior to the performance of the *Seraglio* (*TK,* 230). He is singing the first verse of the song entitled *Parted* (1899), with words by Frederick E "Fred" Weatherly (1848-1929) and music by Sir Francesco Paolo Tosti (1846-1916). Weatherly was an Oxford-educated lawyer (King's Counsel) who combined success in that profession with the writing of song lyrics and children's books. He is said to have written lyrics for over 3,000 songs, including such popular favourites as *Danny Boy* and *Roses of Picardy,* as well as the hymn, *The Holy City,* and English translations of the operas *Pagliacci* and *Cavalleria Rusticana.* Tosti was an Italian-born composer and music teacher who settled in England where he became, for a time, one of its most successful composers of popular songs. He also achieved social and academic distinction with his appointments as singing master to the Royal Family and professor at the Royal Academy of Music. He became a British citizen and was made a knight by Edward VII before returning to Italy where he died in Rome. Some of his songs (including *Goodbye, Mattinata, Serenata* and the Neapolitan song *Marechiare,* as well as the one intoned by Moreland in the novel) are still included in the repertory of many singers of classical music.

Death and Transfiguration
[See STRAUSS, Richard.]

DEBUSSY, Claude (1862-1918)
French composer whose impressionist music at the turn of the century represented the transition from the 19th century late-romantic to the 20th century modern (*CCR,* 63). [See also *L'Après-midi d'un faune, Iberia, Martyrdom of Saint Sebastian, Pelléas et Mélisande.*]

DELIUS, Frederick (1862-1934)
English-born composer of German parentage (originally named Fritz Theodor Albert Delius), he lived and worked in Florida, Germany, Norway and France. He changed his name to Frederick after settling in France in 1897 where he remained for the rest of his life. British conductor Sir Thomas Beecham (1879-1961) championed Delius' music and was the organizer of a

Delius Festival in 1929. This consisted of six concerts, most of which were performed at Queen's Hall, London (*qv.*). It is probably this festival that Maclintick and Gossage discuss at the Mortimer in a scene which would have taken place in about 1929 (*CCR*, 23).

DIAGHILEV, Serge (1872-1929)
Russian art critic and ballet impresario who founded the dance company *Ballets Russes* in 1909. [See Russian Ballet.]

"Di, Di, in her collar and tie" **
Cabaret song sung in a "shrill, hesitant voice, like that of an elderly governess" by Max Pilgrim (*qv.*) accompanied by Heather Hopkins (*qv.*) at Dicky Umfraville's night club. Jeavons compares it unfavourably with the songs of his younger days. "God knows what it's all about, for one thing" (*LM*, 185-86). A bit later, however, Peter Templer, when asked about the Pilgrim-Hopkins performance, declares it "frightfully old-fashioned ... The only reason they are here is because their act was a flop at the Café de Madrid" (*LM*, 190). The song is recollected by Jenkins while on leave during the war when he re-encounters Dicky Umfraville, now engaged to Frederica Tolland, at Frederica's house. "I had to agree that night-clubs seemed the characteristic background for our past encounters" (*VB*, 140-41). [See also *WN*, 67.]

Divisional Concert **
This is an annual affair organized by the officer in charge of the Mobile Laundry Unit. Bithel falls heir to this position, at least in part because "some threads of Thespian prestige" still cling to him as a result of his having somewhat exaggerated the importance of his position for a few months as "front of the house" in a provincial theatre just prior to its conversion into a cinema. In his role as producer and director of the Divisional Concert, Bithel manages to mount "a very tolerable show", despite taking over on short notice in the middle of rehearsals when his predecessor went sick (*SA*, 9). Sergeant Ablett (also attached to the Mobile Laundry) is known for his star turn at these concerts, where he would "sing forgotten songs, crack antediluvian jokes and dance unrestrainedly about the stage wearing only his underclothes" (*SA*, 217, 223-24). Stringham's assignment to the Mobile Laundry Unit raises hopes that he will appear at the Concert, where he "might even bring off a vocalist's stage debut, something he used to talk of on the strength of having been briefly in the choir at school"; but the unit leaves for the Far East before Stringham gets his chance (*SA*, 170).

In his memoirs, Powell recalls a similar tradition of an annual Divisional Concert that was organized in real life by the officer in charge of the Mobile Bath Unit. During his duty as assistant Camp Commandant at Divisional HQ in Belfast, Powell recounts the story of how a Colonel sent anonymously to the Bath Officer lyrics he had written for the concert hoping he would be recognized as the source. The Bath Officer did in fact recognize the Colonel's handwriting, but contrary to the latter's expectation, the lyrics were consigned to the wastepaper basket and the story publicized throughout the formation (*Faces,* 105-07).

DOLLY SISTERS
Twin-sister vaudeville dance act consisting of Rosika (Rosie) and Jansci (Jenny) Deutsch, born in Hungary in 1892 and emigrated to the US with their family in 1905. Starting in 1907, they performed a single-sex "tandem" dance act, perfected through practice in front of mirrors. They appeared in the Ziegfeld Follies for two seasons starting in 1911 and later were featured in several films between 1913 and 1920. In 1920 and 1921 they appeared in four major revues in London, which may be where Templer and Stringham encountered them. Just before coming upon Le Bas on their Sunday afternoon excursion, Templer and Stringham discuss the sisters' ages, with Stringham maintaining that one was the mother of the other (*QU,* 38). At that time (Summer 1922), the sisters would both have been 29. Jenny committed suicide in 1941 and Rosie attempted to do so in 1962 but lived on until 1970.

Don Juan
In a discussion between Barnby and Moreland regarding the differences between Casanova (*qv.*) and Don Juan, Moreland cites *Don Juan* – the opera – as evidence for differences in their characters. "Don Juan merely liked power ... He obviously did not know what sensuality was ... Casanova, on the other hand, undoubtedly had his sensual moments" (*CCR,* 34-35). [See also *WN,* 77 ("Don Juans ... are never in love at all, except with themselves").]

The opera to which Moreland refers is almost certainly *Don Giovanni* (Italian for Don Juan) by Mozart (*qv.*) first performed in 1787. Don Juan is also the principal character in the 1819-24 poem of that title by Lord Byron and in the Spanish play *Don Juan Tenorio.* [See SPURLING, Book Index.] [See also *Faust.*]

A similar discussion takes place among some of the characters in Powell's last novel, *The Fisher King* (1986), in which another character (Mr Jack) is compared to the Don Juan model (although no mention is made in that discussion of Casanova) (*FK,* 114-17).

DVOŘÁK, Antonin (1841-1904)
Czech composer mentioned by Nick Jenkins at the wartime performance of Smetana's *The Bartered Bride* as the other great national composer of the Czechs, apparently overlooking Leoš Janáček (1854-1928), the third member of the Czech musical triumvirate. Colonel Hlava notes that Dvořák was a poor man, like Smetana, and that his father was a pork butcher who also

played bagpipes in the mountains, "like in Scotland". Other sources indicate that Dvořák's father played the zither professionally (*MP*, 98).

ELGAR, Edward (1857-1934)
English composer. At the Victory Thanksgiving Service in St Paul's the Welsh Guards "strummed away at Holst, Elgar, Grieg and finally Handel's „Water Music'." One of the attachés beats time to the music, and it occurs to Jenkins that "Moreland would have only partially approved" (*MP*, 218).

According to the service sheet, "Nimrod" from his *Enigma Variations,* is the work by Elgar that was played at the Victory Service. It was also played as the organ prelude at Powell's Memorial Service. The full name of this work is *Variations on an Original Theme for Orchestra* (Op. 36) and "Nimrod" is Variation No. 9 (Adagio) of the 14 variations of the complete work. Elgar's music in this piece is a variation he intended to be "in the style of" music from Beethoven's *Sonata No. 8 (Pathétique).* Each variation is dedicated to a particular friend of the composer, and No. 9 is dedicated to his closest friend, Augustus Jaeger. The name "Nimrod" is a pun on Jaeger's surname, Nimrod being an Old Testament patriarch and a well-known hunter, which is the meaning of *"jaeger"* in German. The work was composed by Elgar in 1898-99 and first performed at St James's Hall, London in 1899.

The Embassy Club or The Embassy
London night club at 6-8 Old Bond Street, W1 that thrived in the 1920s-30s, was run, at least in its early days, by a man named Luigi and was the venue for performances of well known dance bands of that era. [See Ambrose and *Balls, Picnics and Parties.*] Stringham tells Mrs Andriadis he is leaving her party to go to this club even though she reminds him that it will be closed (*BM*, 144).

ENSA
Abbreviation for Entertainments National Service Association (sometimes said to stand for "Every Night Something Awful"), an organization established in 1939 to provide entertainment for the British troops during WWII. Max Pilgrim is working for ENSA in 1941 (according to Moreland, "entertaining the forces – by his own account enjoying a spot of entertainment himself") when he is released to do a brief season at the Café de Madrid (*qv.*) (*SA*, 116).

Die Entführung aus dem Serail
Opera (K. 384) by WA Mozart (*qv.*) first produced at the command of Emperor Joseph II (1741-90, reigned 1765-90) and performed at the Burgtheater in Vienna in 1782 (at the time, known as *"Teutsches Nationaltheater"*). The opera is known in English as *Abduction from the Seraglio*, although in *Dance* it is referred to in English as simply *Seraglio*.

The opera is written in three acts in the form of a *Singspiel*, with much of the action spoken rather than sung. The plot involves the kidnapping of Konstanze (betrothed to Belmonte, a Spanish nobleman) and her English maid, Blonde, by pirates who sell them to a Turk, Pasha Selim. His servant, Osmin, also has a prominent role and sings the bass part. The women are in the process of being rescued from the Pasha's Seraglio by Belmonte and his servant, Pedrillo, when they are caught in the act by Osmin and returned to the Pasha. Osmin is overjoyed at his success and gloats over his "triumph". The Pasha, however, even though he discovers that Belmonte is the son of a man who treated him cruelly, overcomes the impulse for revenge and releases both couples, teaching them all a lesson in humanity. He seems to be Mozart's embodiment of the ideals of the Enlightenment.

The work includes what are described as some of Mozart's most spectacular, complex and difficult arias, not least Osmin's aria in Act III (*"Ho, how will I triumph"*; originally *"Ha, wie will ich triumphieren"*) that twice goes down to a low D, said to be the lowest note demanded of any voice in opera. There is an anecdote associated with the opera in which the Emperor Joseph II comments, "That is too fine for my ears – there are too many notes" to which Mozart is said to have replied (in some versions) "There are just as many notes as there should be", or (in others) "There are an extraordinary number of notes".

The opera is staged in *TK* as a charity performance arranged by Odo and Rosie Stevens in a tent theatre on the roof of their house in Regent's Park (*TK,* 224 ff.). Moreland provides advice on the production (but does not direct the orchestra in the book as he does in the Channel 4 TV film in which several brief selections from the opera are performed). His name isn't on the programme. Jenkins remarks that Moreland's participation was "unexpected" due both to his failing health and his usual disinclination to support charity performances. Years earlier, however, at the party arranged to celebrate the premiere of his symphony, Moreland states that he once "conducted a charity concert" in the Manaschs' house, apparently referring to a concert arranged by Rosie's parents, who were also patrons of the arts (*CCR,* 177 and *BDFR,* 100). He agreed to participate in this instance because of his love for African art (although not necessarily one of the African causes benefited by the performance of the opera). According to Powell's memoirs, Constant Lambert also preferred the arts of Asia and Africa to those of the High Renaissance favoured by Powell (*Messengers,* 59). Audrey Maclintick, who accompanies Moreland, believes he may also have offered his help because of his having known "Mrs Stevens in what he loves to call The Old Days" (*TK,* 226-27).

In the interval following the Second Act (in which "took place, the drunken scenes, the setting to rest of fears that the girls might join the Pasha's harem")

Moreland discusses the opera with fellow musical associates Gossage (still a critic) and Chandler (now no longer dancing and acting, but a director). Moreland expresses his fondness for the English maid, Blonde, finding her "vixenish touch sympathetic". Chandler favours Osmin, leading Gossage to giggle since he feels the singer is "more of a baritone than a bass". Gossage also comments that "some cardinal appoggiaturas went west in the last Act" (*TK,* 226, 237), referring to vocal ornaments that are typically one step above or below the preceding note and indicated in the score as small notes. As they leave the party after the performance, Gossage remarks to Chandler that he thinks there was "a nice turn of power in the middle notes ... A fine sensibility of phrase" and asks Chandler if he doesn't agree, to which Chandler merely responds with an expression of concern over Moreland's health (*TK,* 247-48).

"Everything is buzz-buzz now"
Popular song overheard on a gramophone at the refreshments shack where Stringham, Templer and Jenkins stop for a ginger-beer after their encounter with Le Bas while on their Sunday afternoon walkabout (*QU,* 44). This is a song from the 1918 London revue *Buzz-Buzz* produced by André Charlot (1882-1956) who is known as the originator of the "intimate revue" and is credited with the discovery of Bea Lillie and Gertrude Lawrence (although other sources also claim that CB Cochran (*qv.*) deserves credit for their discovery). The words of this song were written by English librettist Ronald Jeans (1887-1973) with music by Russian-born British bandleader-composer Herman Darewski (1883-1947). The revue opened on 20 December 1918 at the Vaudeville Theatre and ran for 612 performances. The song appeared in the revue as the finale to Act 1 and was performed by Walter Williams, the heart-throb of the piece. He also made a recording of the song which was still in circulation in 1922 according to Columbia Records UK catalogue for that year (Columbia L1294). It was probably his recording that is overheard by Jenkins, Stringham and Templer as Stringham springs the trap that catches Le Bas in the "Braddock alias Thorne" incident. The flip side of the recording contains Williams' rendition of the US hit song *K-K-K-Katy* which was also included in Charlot's revue and is still fairly well known. Powell mentions that song being whistled by an Eton student he witnesses on his first day at the school as exhibiting "an almost perfect specimen of the Eton Slouch ... the most sophisticated thing [Powell] had ever seen". [See Anthony Powell, "The Watr'y Glade" (1934) in Graham Greene (ed.), *The Old School* (Oxford, 1984 edition), 127-28.]

Existential Music
Moreland is asked by Bagshaw to write an article on this topic for *Fission.* Even though Moreland suspects himself of existential tendencies, he refuses Bagshaw's offer, concluding that he has "turned his back on contemporary

life". He also recalls Maclintick's observation that a musician's life remains all but unchanged by the circumstances of the period in which he lives. Quoting Ben Jonson's preference for the modern where the poet farts upon the "stale and antick" Euclid, Moreland says he himself has it the other way around, and is more inclined to "break wind" upon the Moderns. He then asks to be forgiven for

> *sneering at Youth ... High pitched voices adumbrating absolute values, rational states of mind, intellectual integrity, civilised personal relationships, significant form ... the Fitzroy Street Barbera is uncorked. Le Sacre du Printemps [qv.] turned on, a hand slides up a leg ... All are at one now, values and lovers.*
> (*BDFR*, 118-19)

Moreland's discourse here recalls Constant Lambert's description of the "immense prestige" enjoyed by *Le Sacre du Printemps*

> *with a certain type of intellectual ... due to the fact that it is barbaric music for the supercivilized, an aphrodisiac for the jaded and surfeited.*
> (Constant Lambert, *Music Ho!* (London, 1985 edition), 51)

"Fading is the world's best pleasure"
Line from the hymn *Glorious Things of Thee are Spoken*, appearing at the end of the final verse:

> *Fading is the worldling's pleasure,*
> *All his boasted pomp and show,*
> *Solid joys and lasting treasure*
> *None but Zion's children know.*

At the Victory Thanksgiving Service, Jenkins recalls Stringham's description of this line as "a wonderful statement" in which "one sees very clearly which particular pleasure its writer considered the best" (*MP*, 222). Stringham gets the words confused, replacing "worldling's" with "world's best". That confusion is necessary, however, to support the interpretation adopted by Stringham of the hymn writer's intention. This hymn was also sung at the close of Powell's funeral service at Holy Trinity Church, Chantry, Somerset on 4 April 2000.

The words were written by John Newton (1725-1807) an English ex-slave trader, turned "born again" Christian, who also wrote the words to the hymn *Amazing Grace*, in which the reference to the "wretch like me ... [who] once was lost, but now am found" is, no doubt, autobiographical. *Glorious Things* is most often sung to the tune *Austria*, written in 1797 by Austrian composer Franz Josef Haydn (1732-1809) for the birthday of Emperor Francis II (1768-1835, reigned 1792-1835). The melody, based on a Croatian tune, was the official Austrian *"Volkshymne"* from 1797 to 1918, and was also used by the first Austrian Republic, becoming the Austrian national anthem in 1929 and, again, for a brief period after 1945. The tune was also adopted as the German national anthem in 1922 (*Das Deutschlandlied* or *Das Lied der Deutschen*) with words by German poet Hoffman von Fallersleben (1798-1874) first performed in 1841. His intention was to replace the words of the Austrian *Volkshymne*, associated with the Hapsburgs, by a Pan-German hymn. The first verse with the familiar opening lines *"Deutschland, Deutschland, über alles | Über alles in der Welt"* was the official version in the Nazi period but was replaced in 1952 with the less imperialistic lines of the third stanza *"Einigkeit und Recht und Freiheit | Für das Deutsche Vaterland"* ("Unity, justice and freedom | For the German Fatherland"). The hymn is also sung to other tunes, but *Austria* would likely have been the one known to Stringham.

Famous conductor **
Of "a generation older than Moreland's", who attends Mrs Foxe's party for Moreland's symphony.

> *This distinguished person was conversing a little loudly and self-consciously, with a great deal of gesticulation, to show there was no question of condescension from himself towards his less successful colleagues.* (*CCR*, 142, 161, 187)

FARINELLI (1705-82)
Stage name of Italian opera singer, Carlo Broschi, the most famous *castrato* of the 18th century. Also the name of Moreland's large (presumably neutered) tabby cat (*KO,* 98, 240).

Faust
On the night of the *"Seven Deadly Sins"* at Stourwater, Donners tells Moreland that he had been to a performance of *Faust* at which he thought some of the singing was disappointing (*KO,* 116). He is probably referring to the opera by Charles Gounod (*qv.*) first performed in 1859 with a libretto based on Johann Wolfgang Goethe's (1749-1832) *Faust, Part I.* During the war, Jenkins sees himself playing a role in this opera when he urges Gwatkin, against the latter's judgment, to pursue his love for Maureen the barmaid. Gwatkin's reaction is described in operatic terms:

> *He looked at me astonished. I felt a shade uncomfortable, rather like Mephistopheles unexpectedly receiving a hopelessly negative reaction from Faust. Such an incident in opera, I thought, might suggest a good basis for an aria.* (*VB*, 191)

As it turns out, Gwatkin takes Jenkins' Mephistophelian advice, and it contributes to his downfall, at least insofar as advancement in the army is concerned. In a later novel, Jenkins wonders whether Gwinnett's personality suits him to play the role of Faust, while Glober's would be more suitable to Don Juan in operatic terms of reference (*TK,* 139). In the pre-war novel *From a View to a Death* (1933), Zouch, the *übermensch*, catches sight of local beauty, Joanna Brandon, during a church service and is reminded of "the cathedral scene in *Faust*" (*FVD,* 44).

The Fire-Watcher's March **
[See MORELAND: Works.]

FOKINE, Michel (1880-1942)
[See Russian Ballet.]

"Follow, follow, we will follow Davies (or Gwatkin)"
First line of the refrain from the 19th century Revivalist hymn *Down In the Valley With My Saviour I Would Go*, words by William Orcutt Cushing (1823-1902) and music by Robert W Lowry (1826-99): "Follow, follow, I would follow Jesus". Also adopted with different words by supporters of Glasgow Rangers FC as their team song.

Bithel sings this refrain twice, both times referring to an earlier incident involving a well-remembered (by him) romp after a Christmas dinner in the Regimental Mess. There is no other record of this incident in the novel. Since Bithel is unlikely to have been either a Rangers supporter (although he was rumoured to have played rugby football for Wales) or a hymn-singing Revivalist, there may also have circulated a soldiers' version of the song. He first sings it ("in a thin piping voice, not unlike Max Pilgrim's") while Jenkins and Stringham are trying to guide him home after finding him on the street much the worse for drink, and later, after Widmerpool appears on the scene, in "a lower key than before". On those occasions he sings that he will follow Colonel Davies (*SA,* 180, 184). Many years later, when Bithel ("in a state of extreme intoxication") meets Jenkins and Barnabas Henderson at the latter's London gallery to deliver Stringham's Modigliani drawing, he sings this song in a gentle voice but confuses Gwatkin with Davies, probably because Jenkins has asked him just previously if he remembers Gwatkin in order to bring his attention into focus (*HSH,* 265).

Fox-trot
A ballroom dance which may have taken its name from its US-born originator Harry Fox, stage name of Arthur Carringford (1882-1959). The dance-step had its premiere in 1914 in a New York vaudeville show in which appeared both Fox and, *inter alia*, the Dolly Sisters (*qv.*), to one of whom (Jenny) he was briefly married. The step was later popularized after it was taken up by the exhibition dancers, Vernon and Irene Castle. The step, which consisted of slow-slow-quick-quick 4/4 rhythmic movements, was more flexible than, and

ultimately replaced the one-step and two-step. Jenkins is introduced to the dance by Lady McReith on a visit to Peter Templer's family home:

> *Lady McReith suddenly jumped up from the sofa, took my arm and, sliding it round her waist, danced a few steps ... and then as she continued to cling to me, tracing her steps back in the other direction.*

This experience opens up to Jenkins a whole new realm of the not inconsiderable possibilities that life might hold (*QU*, 91-92). The music is provided by an unidentified gramophone record.

Powell's description of Jenkins' first experience of these new possibilities opened up by dancing the fox-trot has some basis in his own adventures as a youth in Paris, as described in his memoirs. During the Long Vacation of 1925, Powell went with a male traveling companion to a tea-shop *cum* dance-hall on the *Champs-Elysées* where you could "take tea (or a drink), and foxtrot all afternoon. Everyone was dancing-mad at that epoch, the *thé-dansant* all the rage". He succeeds in attracting the attentions of a "small decidedly pretty girl" who agrees to meet him at the same venue the next afternoon. She turns out, however, to be a tart (Lulu), and at the end of their rendezvous (which extended well beyond the dance-hall) Powell "felt considerable nervous exhaustion, though in principle better able to face the world" (*Infants,* 176-77).

"*From every dark nook they press forward to meet me*" (*The Ash Grove*)
Lines from the last verse of *The Ash Grove*. [See "My lips smile no more, my heart loses its lightness".]

Funiculì, Funiculà
Italian song, words by Italian journalist Peppino Turco and music by Italian composer Luigi Denza (1846-1922) written in 1880 on the occasion of the opening of the funicular railway on Mount Vesuvius. The song became so closely associated with Italian popular culture in the 19th century, that Richard Strauss (*qv.*), thinking it a folk song, incorporated it into his symphonic poem *Aus Italien*, first performed in 1887, only to face a lawsuit from the composer Denza as a result of which Strauss was required to pay a royalty each time his piece was performed in public.

The song is heard by Nick Jenkins as he sits alongside the Grand Canal in Venice and is performed by an elderly member of a troupe of street (or canal) musicians at the beginning of *TK*. He is reminded of having heard the same song 40 or 50 years earlier at the same spot adjacent to the same hotel and wonders if it is the same musician, who applied similar gestures:

With an operatic out-thrust of the body, he intimated the Kingdoms
of the earth ranged beneath the funicular passengers for their
delectation.

The musician's "stylized movements" remind Jenkins of Dicky Umfraville's impersonations and trigger an interior monologue about Umfraville and his latter-day descent into melancholy (*TK,* 1-4). [See also STREET MUSICIANS: Old Venetian singer.]

The words of the song as transcribed by Jenkins differ from the original lyrics in Neapolitan dialect. For example, the original Neapolitan version

Se vede Francia, Proceta e la Spagna
Io veco a tte

is heard by Jenkins (and perhaps sung by the Venetian musicians) as

Si vede Francia, Procida, la Spagna
E io veggo te

which more closely approximates Italian as spoken north of Naples. Later on, Dr Brightman expatiates on the difficulty of transferring Neapolitan popular music to the north. [See *Santa Lucia*.]

The song continues to recur as a *leitmotif* throughout the first chapter of *TK.* Jenkins is reminded of the aged singer when he sees the outdated photograph of Ferrand-Sénéschal in Gwinnett's copy of the French "true detective" newspaper which promises, but does not deliver lurid details of the Frenchman's recent death. The photo catches him in a passionate gesture with his hands above his head "as if he, too, were singing *Funiculì, Funiculà,* miming the ascending cable" (*TK,* 44). Jenkins later hears the musicians' refrain in the distance from his hotel room as he retires for the night, although the cadences might have then "wafted synthetically from the radio" (*TK,* 51). At the close of the chapter, Jenkins is again reminded of the ancient singer when he thinks of meeting the slightly less senior Tokenhouse while the singer's voice "or another's echoed on that summer night" the words of *Funiculì, Funiculà* (*TK,* 59). In a final, less musical allusion, Jenkins describes the painting of *Candaules and Gyges* as exhibiting a view "far outdoing anything to be glimpsed from the funicular" and thought it "seemed Venetian rather than Neapolitan in feelings" (*TK,* 83).

God Save the King (National Anthem)
First three verses are sung at conclusion of the Victory Thanksgiving Service. It is the national anthem of the United Kingdom and is formally called *God Save the King/Queen.* On official occasions, only the first verse is sung, occasionally the third; so, the singing of the second verse (more recently deleted for reasons of "political correctness" but which Jenkins regards as

"incidentally much the best") marks the patriotic importance of the occasion (*MP*, 226-27). Bob Duport remarks that one of the reasons he never "really hit it off" with Jean Templer when they were married was because of her limited knowledge of music; "she only knew *God Save the King* because everybody stood up" (*MP*, 190).

The origin of the words and music is shrouded in confusion and controversy, and in some circles it is preferred that its source be referred to as "anonymous" or "traditional" or merely "17th or 18th century". It seems to be generally agreed that a published version appeared in 1744 and that it was performed and achieved initial popularity in 1745, in coincidence with the landing in Scotland of Charles Edward Stuart. This may account for the concluding lines of the now suppressed sixth and final verse of the original:

> *May he sedition hush*
> *And like a torrent rush,*
> *Rebellious Scots to crush.*
> *God save the King!*

These lines may also explain why Scotland does not use this hymn as its national anthem.

The tune also served for the unofficial national anthem of the German Empire from 1871 to 1918 and before that, the Prussian Empire: *Heil dir im Siegerkranz; Hail to thee in victor's crown.* The tune was also adopted as the national anthem of other nations, as well as a patriotic song in the US (*My Country 'Tis of Thee*) and a hymn in some Protestant churches.

Anyone wishing to delve more deeply into the source of this hymn would do well to consult the entry by Percy Scholes in the *Oxford Companion to Music*.

GOSSAGE **
Weekly music critic, friend of Moreland and Maclintick.

> *A lean toothy little man, belonging to another common musical*
> *type. He toyed nervously with his bow tie, pince-nez and*
> *moustache, the last of which carried little conviction of masculinity.*

Voice "like a ventriloquist's doll" (*CCR*, 19). Finds Norman Chandler a "talented young gentleman". Discusses an Albert Hall concert and the Delius Festival at the Queen's Hall with Maclintick (*CCR*, 22-23). Likes Moreland's symphony (*CCR*, 150), but "barely civil" about *Tone Poem Vieux Port* (*SA*, 135). Critical of the bass performing in the *Seraglio*. "The man's more of a baritone than a bass. Some cardinal appoggiaturas went west in the last Act, I'm afraid" (*TK*, 237). Later he notes a "nice turn of power in the middle notes" (*TK*, 247).

GOUNOD, Charles-François (1818-1893)

French composer best known for his operas. Jenkins overhears General Conyers playing Gounod's *Ave Maria* (*qv.*) on his 'cello when he visits the Conyers' flat at Sloane Square (*LM,* 69-70). When Jenkins revisits the Sloane Square flat at the beginning of the war, the General, now a widower, is said to be still playing Gounod (*KO,* 208). Jenkins during the war is reminded of General Conyers' rendition of this music by an air raid warning, recalling "some musical instrument inadequately mastered" (*SA,* 6). [See also *WN,* 84.]

GRIEG, Edvard (1843-1907)

Norwegian composer. His *Lyric Suite* is listed among the pieces played by the Welsh Guards at the Victory Thanksgiving Service. [See also ELGAR.] This probably refers to the *Lyric Suite for Orchestra,* Opus 54. It was initially written in 1891 for piano but was orchestrated by Grieg in 1904. It consists of four pieces, the most well-known of which is *March of the Trolls.* Grieg's *Ave Maris Stella* (hymn to Mary, *Hail, Star of the Sea,* Opus 150 of 1893 is a choral work that was performed at Powell's Memorial Service.

Guide Me, O Thou Great Jehovah (*Cwm Rhondda*)

Hymn published in Welsh by William Williams (1717-91) – also known as Williams Pantycelyn or simply Pantycelyn – in 1745 and published in an English translation by Peter Williams (1723-96) in 1771. The hymn tune was written by John Hughes (1873-1932) to conform to the previously written words and was first performed, according to one source, in about 1907 in a chapel located in the Rhondda Valley ("*Cwm Rhondda*" in Welsh) of South Wales. According to a BBC website, Welsh hymn tunes were often named for the places where they were written to enable itinerant organists to play tunes instantly recognizable by name, allowing the congregation to join in with whatever version of the words they knew. Another source claims that Hughes composed it in 1905 for a Welsh song festival.

The first verse of the hymn is sung by "the whole Battalion" as it marches to the transport taking it from Wales to Northern Ireland.

> *The singing on the march, whatever form it took, always affirmed*
> *the vicissitudes of life, the changes, so often for the worse, that*
> *beset human experience, especially in the army, especially in time*
> *of war.* (VB, 39-40)

[See also *Faces,* 102.]

Another verse ("When I tread the verge of Jordan") is sung quietly to himself by Lance-Corporal Gittins (*VB,* 102). What is usually the second verse ("Open now the crystal fountain") is sung by soldiers being transported to divisional hospital in the truck that carries Jenkins to his new assignment at Division HQ (*VB,* 237) and again when Jenkins happens upon units of his former Division in Belgium during the tour of the Military Attachés (*MP,* 177). In his memoirs, Powell says the Belgian encounter actually took place, although whether the hymn-singing was also factual is not stated (*Faces,* 171).

Years later, at Stourwater, outside the Akworth-Cutts wedding, a voice bursts out singing the "crystal fountain" verse in thin, quavering notes, startling Widmerpool who urges the assembled guests and cult members to take no notice. The song reminds Jenkins of his Regiment, but he fails to recognize the ancient, dishevelled, grey-bearded singer until he is revealed by Widmerpool to be Bithel (*HSH,* 215-17). Later, as the wedding party is breaking up, Bithel sings the "verge of Jordan" verse "in a high, quavering [voice], much enhanced by champagne". The hymn is echoed briefly "by another chant, possibly Umfraville's – he had served in the Welsh Guards" (*HSH,* 238).

In his memoirs Powell remarks that, when it fell to him to choose the hymns for George Orwell's funeral in 1950, he included *Guide Me, O Thou Great Redeemer,* the words appearing in the Anglican hymnal, while admitting that "chiefly from my own wartime associations, *Jehovah* is more authentic". (*Faces,* 221). In his *Journals* Powell also offered the same comment when the hymn was sung at the 1988 funeral of his friend Tanya Hobson (*J87-89,* 108). The more authentic version was sung by the congregation as the opening hymn at Powell's own funeral service at Holy Trinity Church, Chantry, Somerset on 4 April 2000 and as the closing hymn at his Memorial Service at the Grosvenor Chapel in London on 4 May 2000.

HANDEL, George Frideric (1685-1759)
German-born composer who lived most of his life in England, becoming an English citizen by Royal Assent in 1727. Perhaps because of his long residence in England and his strong Protestantism, much of his music has patriotic associations with his adopted land; indeed, some of his favourite works (*eg. Water Music (qv.)* and *Music for the Royal Fireworks,* HWV 351, 1749) were commissioned by or dedicated to members of the English Royal Family (many of whom were, at that time, also of German origin).

Priscilla Tolland suggests Handel's *"Cradle Song"* as being preferable to the military music played on the gramophone in the early morning hours by the first husband of a friend of Audrey Maclintick (*CCR,* 174). She probably meant to refer to Brahms' *Cradle Song,* which is a name frequently applied to that composer's *Wiegenlied* or *Lullaby* (Opus 49, No. 4, 1868). There are several pieces by Handel that might be considered appropriate cradle songs – *eg.* a movement of his *Music for the Royal Fireworks* known as *"La Paix"* or *"Largo alla Siciliana"*; the aria *"Già l'ebro mio ciglio"* from his opera *Orlando*; or the aria *"Ombra mai fu"* from his opera *Xerxes.* However, none of these pieces is generally known as a cradle song and would, in any event, unlikely be known to or deemed as such by Priscilla, who is said to have little interest in music. [See also ELGAR and *Messiah*.]

In his pre-*Dance* novel *What's Become of Waring* (1939) Powell mentions Handel's *Where'er you walk* as a work sung by the choir at the wedding which takes place in the novel's opening scene (*WBW*, 2). This same work was performed at Powell's own wedding a few years previously. It was not intended as a choral work but was written as an aria to be sung by the character of Jupiter in Act 2, Scene 3 of Handel's opera *Semele* – apparently to seduce the unsuspecting Semele. The opera, with libretto written previously by English playwright William Congreve (1670-1729), amplified by Alexander Pope (1688-1744), was first performed at the Theatre Royal in London in 1744 and remained relatively neglected until 1925 when it received a stage revival in Cambridge.

"He ran a pin | In Gwendolyn, | In Lower Grosvenor Place"
Jeavons, "now in his most lively mood", recalls a song going something like this after dancing with Mildred Haycock at Umfraville's night club, but he "can't remember the words exactly" (*LM*, 201). It is, in fact, another song remembered by Jeavons (fairly accurately, as it turns out) from his WWI days. The words are from the third verse of a song entitled *Piccadilly* that was included in the musical *Mr Manhattan*, words by dramatic writer Fred Thompson (1884-1929) and CH Bovill (d.1918) and most of the music by Howard Talbot (stage name of Richard Lonsdale Munkittrick, 1865-1928), US-born composer and conductor of many West End musicals. The music for this particular song was by British composer Philip Braham (1881-1934) and the words by actor and lyricist Ralph Roberts (1869-1944). Thompson and Braham were also involved in another of Jeavons' favourite musical plays, *The Bing Boys* (*qv.*), as was George Grossmith Jr, who co-managed the production of *Mr Manhattan*. The West End opening of the play was at the Prince of Wales Theatre on 30 March 1916, where it continued its run for 221 performances, closing on 1 October 1916. The song was also recorded by English stage and screen performer Austin Melford (1884-1971) on HMV C681. The words recalled by Jeavons are sung in the play by the character named Bobby Washington (played by Melford) about a young person named Billy, a rather rakish man-about-town. The complete third verse and chorus go as follows:

> *Billy's awfully keen on figures, and he's somewhat of a judge,*
> *And he prides himself in knowing, which is real and which is fudge,*
> *So he stuck a pin in Gwendolen in Lower Grosvenor Place,*
> *And Gwen, since then, gives Bill the frozen face!*

Chorus:
On his way down Piccadilly, with a filly, not so crazy!
All the boys and girls they chance to meet, say, "who's that comin'
up the street?"
And they shout, "who's that with Billy? Why it's Milly, she's a
daisy!
If you're goin' to Piccadilly, Billy, pick a nice little one for me!"

Powell includes the lines sung by Jeavons in his Notebook (*WN*, 74), spelling
Gwendoline with an „i' and substituting "ran" for "stuck" in the third line, but
otherwise the same as the original. He does not mention where or when he
may have heard the song, however.

HINDEMITH, Paul (1895-1963)
German composer, violist and conductor whose "highbrow" music Moreland
judges would be even less suitable for an early morning gramophone
performance than the military marches complained of by Audrey Maclintick's
friend (*CCR*, 174). [See "*Aut Sousa, aut nihil*".]

HOLST, Gustav (1874-1934)
English composer, best known for his orchestral suite *The Planets* (1916).
His *First Suite in „E' Flat*, Opus 29, No. 1 (1909) is among the pieces played
by the Welsh Guards at the Victory Thanksgiving Service. [See ELGAR.]

HONEGGER, Arthur (1892-1955)
Swiss composer who was born and lived most of his life in France.
Moreland, near the end of his life, recalls writing an article in which he
attacked Honegger and referred in some context to an "apodictic intention" of
that composer, wondering whether „apodictic' was the right word?" (*TK*,
271). He was a member of "*Les Six*" (*qv.*). His best known work is probably
Pacific 231 in which the sound of a steam locomotive is reproduced.

HOPKINS, Heather **
Pianist; plays most nights at the Merry Thought. Has an engagement to
appear with Max Pilgrim at the Café de Madrid (*LM*, 95). Accompanies Max
Pilgrim "vigorously, and with a great deal of facility" at Dicky Umfraville's
club (*LM*, 186). By the end of her career is "giving an imitation of John
Foster Dulles in his galoshes" at the Hero of Acre (*TK*, 31).

"How happy I could be with either" (*The Beggar's Opera*)
Jenkins recalls Moreland's alternative version of this line from a song in *The
Beggar's Opera* when Dr Brightman, in her explication to Pamela of
Candaules and Gyges, refers to "Casanova's divertissement with two nuns
under the eye of Cardinal de Bernis". Moreland had, in an earlier non-
Venetian context, wished for a similar experience to that of Casanova (*qv.*),
causing him to propose the alternative line "How happy I could be with two

girls" (*TK,* 90). The earlier reference was to the discussion in the Mortimer of the differences between Casanova and Don Juan, where Moreland referred to the former's "sensual moments" in which he, unlike Don Juan, enjoyed sexual encounters, such as "those threesomes with the nun, MM" (*CCR,* 35). There is no mention of the song in the earlier passage. In his memoirs, Powell provides a more extended discussion of Casanova's encounters with the two nuns, CC and MM. Indeed, Powell was so absorbed with this sequence of Casanova's *Memoirs* that he sought out the Venetian site of the nuns' residence at the dilapidated (in 1972) and remote conventual church of Santa Maria degli Angeli on the island of Murano, which still retained "a crumbling dignity" (*Strangers,* 88-89).

The Beggar's Opera was written by English poet and playwright John Gay (1685-1732) and first produced at Lincoln's Inn Fields in 1728. It was a "ballad opera" equally dividing spoken dialogue with song. The music was based on traditional or popular music of the times, likely well known to the audience. The music for the song may have been arranged by German-born composer Johann Christoph Pepusch (1667-1752) who is thought to have arranged the overture and may have also arranged the airs. In the opera, the song parodied by Moreland is sung by the character Macheath in Act II, Scene 13, as he is berated by two of the female characters, Lucy and Polly, for having scorned them both:

How happy could I be with either
Were t'other dear Charmer away
But while you thus teaze me together
To neither a word will I say

The original tune for this song was also used for various other popular songs of the day. The play also included a version of the song *Lillibullero.* [See *The Popular Song from Lilliburlero to Lili Marlene.*]

In his memoirs Powell assigns particular importance to a revival of this play which he attended at the Lyric Theatre, Hammersmith in summer 1920 in a production which ran for over 1400 performances. He was especially impressed by the costumes and sets designed by English artist and designer Claud Lovat Fraser (1890-1921) which "brought about something of a minor revolution in his own line", his influence quickly entering "every branch of daily life". Perhaps unknown to Powell, Lovat Fraser did the designs in only four days due to budgetary constraints on the producers.

In addition, Powell concluded that John Gay's libretto also reflects "wit and economy of language [that remained] altogether untarnished after two hundred and fifty years". The opera's

> *mood was perfectly adjusted to that of the Twenties [with]*
> *sentimentality ... suddenly cut short by a call to order*
> *demonstrating the absurdity, savagery and pointlessness of life.*

As an example he recalls the song *Over the Hills and Far Away* which he found "at once sexually and romantically exciting in a way that was altogether new":

Macheath:	*Were I laid on Greenland's Coast,*
	And in my Arms embrac'd my Lass:
	Warm amidst eternal Frost,
	Too soon the half year's Night would pass.

Polly:	*Were I sold on Indian soil,*
	Soon as the burning Day was clos'd,
	I could mock the sultry Toil
	When on my Charmer's Breast repos'd.

| Macheath: | *And I would love you all the Day,* |

| Polly: | *Every Night would kiss and play,* |

| Macheath: | *If with me you'd fondly stray* |

| Polly: | *Over the Hills and far away.* |

These are Gay's lyrics to a traditional song dating back at least to the early 1700's (*Infants*, 88-90). Powell also included a recording of this song among his Desert Island Disc choices in the BBC Radio 4 broadcast of that programme on 16 October 1976. More recently, the song became the theme music for the ITV series about a fictional soldier in the Napoleonic Wars, Richard Sharpe, starting with *Sharpe's Rifles* in 1993. The story is based on books written by Bernard Cornwell (b. 1944).

When Powell took his Balliol Scholarship exams in 1923, one of the examiners at the *viva* (after the written exam had been reviewed) commented to Powell: "You're the fellow who liked *The Beggar's Opera* so much". Powell cannot recall which of the questions elicited answers evidencing his admiration for the play (*Infants*, 145). Powell was not the only writer of his generation to be greatly impressed by the 1920 revival of *The Beggar's Opera*. In his *Diaries*, Evelyn Waugh (1903-1996) recorded no fewer than six visits to performances of the show between January and September 1921, with assessments ranging from "perfect" (4) to "splendid" (1) and "thoroughly good" (1). He also managed to meet Lovat Fraser and later, after he had come down from Oxford, he records meeting the stage manager of the production (Nigel Playfair) and the actress who played Lucy. [See Evelyn Waugh, *Diaries* (London, 1976), 108, 123, 125, 133, 135, 138, 167 n.5, 185.]

A modern version of *The Beggar's Opera* was written by German dramatist Bertolt Brecht (1898-1956) and German composer Kurt Weill (1900-1950) and was first produced in Germany in 1928 as *Die Dreigroschenoper*. English versions of this play entitled *The Threepenny Opera* enjoyed successful runs in New York and London during the 1950's. In his memoirs Powell remarks that

> *some years ago, I saw another revival of The Beggar's Opera [in which] efforts had been made to bring the tone and tunes into line with the fashions of today. Much was lost. (Infants, 89-90).*

Powell's remarks, made in 1976, could refer to any of these productions as well as to revivals of the John Gay version.

In his *Journals* Powell says that he watched a version of *The Beggar's Opera* on television sometime around July 1983 which was also disappointing for many of the same reasons stated in *Infants*. That may have been a television transmission of the 1953 Peter Brook film version, written by Christopher Fry and Denis Cannan and starring Lawrence Olivier as Macheath. He then adds, however, that he saw a TV production of the play on the BBC later that year directed by Dr Jonathan Miller (b. 1934, of *Beyond the Fringe* fame) which he thought so good that he wrote Miller a fan letter. Macheath, as played by pop singer Roger Daltrey (b. 1944) of *The Who*, "was much nearer the mark" (*J82-86*, 73-74). He later mentions that "Daltry [*sic*] is a Lincolnshire name, some of them connected to my mother's family, I think" (*J82-86*, 95). Powell does not mention another connection provided by Daltrey through Constant Lambert (See MORELAND) whose son Christopher "Kit" Lambert (1935-81) was the manager of *The Who*.

"Hugh the Drover"
This is a nickname used by Matilda for Hugh Moreland, "usually when not best pleased with him" (*MP*, 208). It is taken from the name of a character in the opera *Hugh the Drover, or Love in the Stocks* by English composer Ralph Vaughan Williams (1872-1958), set in the Cotswolds in 1812, and first performed at the Royal College of Music, London, in 1924. In what is essentially a love story, the heroine (Mary) and the hero (Hugh the Drover) triumph over opposition to their marriage which at one point sees them locked together in the stocks of the Cotswold town where they meet.

Iberia
The second of three *Images pour orchestre* (Images for Orchestra) by Claude Debussy (*qv.*). *Iberia* consists of three movements, each with Spanish themes: *Par les rues et par les chemins* (By roads and by pathways); *Les parfums de la nuit* (Fragrances of the night); and *Le matin d'un jour de fête* (Feast day morning). These pieces were written over the period 1905-08. Robert Tolland ("rather a keen concert-goer and frequenter of music parties")

plays this music on the gramophone (from which the sounds of Debussy "quavered and tinkled and droned") apropos of the news that his brother Erridge has just announced that he is going to fight in the Spanish Civil War. Jenkins describes the impressions created in his mind by "the sombre, menacing notes adumbrating their Spanish background", mentally converting the music into a series of mostly visual images, concluding with that of Goya's painting *Winter* (*CCR*, 61-63). Thus, even when Jenkins develops a particular interest in a piece of orchestral music, which he (and apparently Powell) did in the case of this work by Debussy, his impressions manifest themselves primarily in the form of visual, not aural, images.

According to a Debussy 78 rpm discography, the only UK recording of *Iberia* before 1936, when this scene in the novel took place, was made in 1927 by the Royal Philharmonic conducted by Paul Klenau (Columbia L1999/2001). There were other recordings by continental orchestras, but it seems more likely that Robert Tolland would have had the Royal Philharmonic version. Columbia Records UK catalogue for 1935 indicates that the Royal Philharmonic version was still available. A three-record 78 rpm set of this version is included among Powell's own surviving record collection. A later recording of this piece was chosen for performance in Powell's "Desert Island Discs" programme.

Idomeneo
Opera seria by Wolfgang Amadeus Mozart (*qv.*) first performed in 1781. Its full name is *Idomeneo, re di Creta ossia Ilia e Idamante* (in English, *Idomeneo, King of Crete or Ilia and Idamante*), but it is almost always referred to as simply *Idomeneo*. The story had previously been set to music as *Idoménée* in 1717 by André Campra but Mozart and librettist Giambattista Varesco were commissioned by Karl Theodor, Elector of Bavaria (1724-99, reigned 1777-99), for a new version. The opera is a topic of conversation at the Walpole-Wilsons' dinner party (*BM*, 35).

If You Were the Only Girl in the World
Song from musical revue *The Bing Boys are Here* (Alhambra Theatre, London, 1916) words by British lyricist Clifford Grey (1887-1941) music by Anglo-American composer of popular music Nat D Ayer (1887-1952). [See also *The Bing Boys*.]

The song was recorded in 1916 (UK Columbia L1035) by the leading performers in the revue, Violet Loraine, British musical theatre actress and singer, née Violet Mary Tipton (1886-1956), and George Robey, stage name of British music hall star George Edward Wade (1869-1954), backed by the Alhambra Theatre Orchestra, John Ansell conducting. Their record was among the selections for Powell's "Desert Island Discs" and may today be played on the internet free of charge. Powell's partiality towards this song was shared by his wife who recalls requesting the band to play it at her debutante ball in 1930, a year in which she describes it as having been among the best of the revivals. [See Powell, Violet, *Five Out of Six* (London, 1960), 231.] The song remained popular for many years thereafter, with another version recorded by Italian-American crooner Perry Como (1912-2001) in 1946.

This is sung by Ted Jeavons "quite loud and in an unexpectedly deep and attractive voice" in Dicky Umfraville's night club upon his recognition of Mildred Haycock (*LM*, 177-78). He later compares Max Pilgrim's song "*Di, Di, in her collar and tie*" (*qv.*) unfavourably to the songs that were prevalent "when I was younger" no doubt having in mind this one which he had sung just previously (*LM*, 186). [See also *WN*, 71.]

In Powell's 1939 novel *What's Become of Waring* the song title becomes part of a joke. In a discussion of a party which took place at the home of what is apparently a Jewish family called the Manasses (*cf.* Manaschs in *Dance*), the narrator mentions to Eustace Bromwich that he saw a mutual female acquaintance at the party, to which Bromwich replies: "I suppose she was the only girl in the world and you were the only *goy*?" (*WBW*, 87).

The song was also sung as a solo at Powell's Memorial Service on 4 May 2000 at the Grosvenor Chapel.

"I'm a trooper, I'm a trooper"
[See BENNETT, Billy.]

In a Persian Market
Light orchestral music by Albert W Ketèlbey (1875-1959), English composer, conductor and pianist. Ketèlbey was trained as a classical musician but became famous for lightweight, popular music, such as this piece. Other music he wrote includes *In a Monastery Garden* (1915), the hit that made him famous. *In a Persian Market* was written in 1920 and has remained popular, recently being used as theme music in a TV commercial. The female orchestra at Café Royal is playing this tune while Jenkins is dining there with Barnby in 1933 and the latter announces "that matters were at an end between Anne Stepney and himself" (*AW*, 172).

"In the mountain greenery"
Lines from the 1926 Rodgers and Hart song *Mountain Greenery*. The correct wording of the lyrics is "*In a mountain greenery*". The song was featured in the second edition of their 1926 Broadway show *Garrick Gaieties* and was included in the London version of *The Girl Friend* (1927). [See *My Heart Stood Still*.] The song is played by one of the competing orchestras performing at balls around Belgrave Square on the "Night of the Three

Parties", while the other is playing *The Blue Room* another Rodgers and Hart show tune (*BM,* 63). [See *"We'll have a Blue Room".*]

JENKINS, Nick **

Claims no special regard for music as that he possesses for other art forms: "music holds for me none of that hard, cold-blooded, almost mathematical pleasure I take in writing and painting" (*CCR,* 15). During his first encounter with Mrs Erdleigh, she asks whether there is a possible musical "link" between them, to which he responds simply "No" (*AW,* 14). When Moreland and his colleagues engage in "musical ‚shop'" talk, Jenkins confesses to "feel rather out of it", or "without feeling – as I came to feel later – that I was, in one sense, part and parcel of the same community" (*CCR,* 23, 25). He claims to have little interest in the "musical politics" which govern Moreland's relations with other musicians, such as Carolo (*CCR,* 156).

Powell similarly says that he himself "lacks musical sensibilities" (*Messengers,* 59). John Monagan, a friend of Powell in his later years, noted that there was little sign of a love of music at Powell's home in Somerset:

> *no piano was in evidence, nor did one see a banjo casually laid aside ... No collection of CDs jostled the vast collection of books on the capacious shelves.*
> [See John S Monagan, "Dance Music", *Anthony Powell Society Newsletter,* **5** (Winter 2001), 4]

He also reports Kingsley Amis' account in his *Memoirs* of a Powell visit to Swansea when Amis began to play a recording of Constant Lambert's *The Rio Grande,* only to have Powell depart to bed when the record was halfway through (*Id.* 6). [See also Amis, Kingsley, *Memoirs* (Penguin Books, 1992), 72, footnote.] Notwithstanding Powell's early bedtime on that occasion, *The Rio Grande* is among the favourites he included in his Desert Island Discs selection.

Jerusalem

Hymn with words by William Blake (1757-1827) from a poem written by him in 1804 and set to music in 1916 by English composer Charles Hubert Hastings Parry (1848-1918) to be sung in that year at a meeting of the "Fight for the Right" women's suffrage organization held in the Queen's Hall (*qv.*). Parry's tune was arranged for orchestra by Sir Edward Elgar (*qv.*) in 1922, and, when King George V (1865-1936, reigned 1910-36) heard that version, he remarked that *Jerusalem* should replace *God Save the King* as the national anthem. To some extent, *Jerusalem* has effectively become an alternative national anthem. It serves, for example, as the official anthem of the Women's Institute, typically sung at the beginning of their meetings, and it is also sung before *God Save the King/Queen* at the Last Night of the Proms (*qv.*).

It was also sung at the Victory Thanksgiving Service. The singing of the hymn causes Jenkins to reflect upon the words by Blake, thinking him a "genius" but at the same time "too cranky". The words "Arrows of desire" remind Jenkins of Abraham Cowley [see SPURLING, Book Index] who was buried in Westminster Abbey, an honour "which would never have happened to Blake", although "it was Blake who had come out on top at the end". General Asbjørnsen "certainly enjoyed singing the words ... [and] was quite flushed in the face, like a suddenly converted Viking, joining in with the monks instead of massacring them" (*MP*, 223-24). The hymn is listed in the service sheet to be sung after the sermon.

John Peel

Traditional English fox-hunting song about a Cumberland farmer, John Peel (circa 1776-1854), who kept a pack of fox hounds. The original words, from about 1829, are by another Cumberland farmer, John Woodcock Graves (circa 1795-1886), who revised them frequently after their first publication in 1865-6, leaving several variations and much controversy, of which more below. It is sung to a traditional tune based, by most accounts, on a Scottish dance (known as a "rant") with the words "*Bonnie Annie*" appearing somewhere in the title. An arrangement of the music was written in 1868 by William Metcalfe, who was lay clerk at Carlisle Cathedral. He sang the song in his version at the 1869 annual dinner of the Cumberland Benevolent Society in London, from whence it achieved its popularity, with printed versions circulated widely. Metcalfe's arrangement for the refrain seems to have become the prevalent version of the tune for the entire song as it is sung today. Both the tune and the words of the song, however, continue to exist in various versions about which some controversies remain unresolved.

The first verse in the preferred version from one of several *John Peel* internet websites goes like this:

> *D'ye ken John Peel with his coat so gay,*
> *D'ye ken John Peel at the break of day,*
> *D'ye ken John Peel when he's far away,*
> *With his hounds and his horn in the morning.*

There is a dispute over whether the coat in line 1 is „gay', „gray' or „grey'. And in some versions (like the one Jenkins recalls in the novel) Peel is „far, far away' in line 3 (which also scans better with the tune now prevalent). Jenkins recalls this verse of the song when he hears of St John Clarke's death: "now, like John Peel, he has gone far, far away, with his pen and his press-clippings in the morning" (*CCR*, 193).

Powell also used lines from the third verse of the song for both the title and epigraph of his 1933 novel, *From a View to a Death*. The controversy over the words of the song also clouded that decision (*Messengers*, 187).

KARSAVINA, Tamara (1885-1978)
[See Russian Ballet.]

Lady Macbeth of the Mtsensk District
[See SHOSTAKOVITSCH.]

LAMBERT, Constant (1905-51)
[See MORELAND: Source.]

LAUDER, Harry (1870-1950)
Stage name of Sir Henry Lauder, Scottish entertainer, singer and songwriter who was dubbed by Winston Churchill "Scotland's greatest ever ambassador". At his peak, he is said to have been the world's highest paid entertainer. He wrote many of his own songs and performed in music halls, films and broadcast media. While on his training course at Aldershot, Jenkins takes part in a drill that is

> *squadded by a stagey cluster of glengarry-capped staff-sergeants*
> *left over from the Matabele campaign, with Harry Lauder accents*
> *and eyes like poached eggs. (VB, 117)*

Lili Marlene
[See *Popular Music from Lilliburlero to Lili Marlene.*]

Lilliburlero
[See *Popular Music from Lilliburlero to Lili Marlene.*]

LISZT, Franz or Ferenc (1811-86)
Hungarian pianist and composer. Moreland's uncle is said to have heard Liszt play at the Crystal Palace (*qv.*), where he had "seen the Abbé's black habit and shock of iron-grey hair pass through Sydenham" to which the Crystal Palace was relocated in 1854 and in which a concert hall was installed in 1857 (*CCR,* 4). Liszt had taken minor religious orders after moving to Rome and became Abbé Liszt in 1865. While the uncle may well have seen Liszt passing through Sydenham, where he stayed in a private home on his last visit to London in 1886, and may have seen him in attendance at either of two concerts in his honour which were performed at Crystal Palace (10 and 17 April 1886), it is unlikely that he heard Liszt play on either of those occasions. Liszt was 75 in 1886 and considered himself to be well past his prime as a performer. He refused to accept any engagements to perform during that 1886 tour, although he did play a few pieces as the spirit moved him at several private and public concerts. His biographer meticulously describes these impromptu performances but does not mention one occurring at either of the Crystal Palace concerts attended by Liszt. [See Alan Walker, *Franz Liszt: Volume 3, The Final Years, 1861-1886* (New York, 1996), 477-

89.] Liszt's previous visit to London had taken place in 1841 before the Crystal Palace existed.

Colonel Hlava, head of the Czechoslovak military mission during the war, has a look of Liszt "about his head and thick white hair, together with a certain subdued air of belonging to the Romantic Movement". This may have been "due to a drop of Hungarian blood ... though Hlava himself claimed entirely Bohemian or Moravian origins" (*MP,* 97). After the war, Carolo's long "snow white" hair also reminds Jenkins of Liszt when Carolo takes a bow after appearing in the orchestra as Second Violinist in the charity performance of *Die Entführung aus dem Serail* (*qv.*) sponsored by Odo and Rosie Stevens (*TK,* 240).

Lohengrin
Opera by Richard Wagner (*qv.*), first performed in 1850. The story is based on the Swan Knight legend as told in the Medieval German romances of Wolfram von Eschenbach, *Parzival* [see *Parsifal*] and its sequel *Lohengrin.* In Act 1, the Swan Knight, *Lohengrin*, a tenor, arrives, carried across the water by a swan to rescue the heroine, Elsa. The opera becomes a topic of conversation at the Walpole-Wilsons' dinner party (*BM,* 35). [See SLEZAK and Wedding March.]

London Pavilion
Building on the northeast side of Piccadilly Circus between Shaftesbury Avenue and Coventry Street. It was originally built as a music hall in 1859, reconstructed in 1923 with electric billboards on its sides, and again in 1934 when it became a cinema. In 1986 it was converted into a shopping arcade with exterior walls preserved, and in 2000 it was connected to the Trocadero (a gambling casino) with the signage changed to London Trocadero (now an entertainment / shopping centre).

CB Cochran was manager of this theatre after its first reconstruction. [See also Mr Cochran's Young Ladies and *"My Heart Stood Still"*.] Moreland encounters the peg-legged street musician playing behind this building in 1941 on his way to meet Nick Jenkins at the nearby Café Royal (*qv.*). [See *"Softly Awakes My Heart"*.]

LORTZING, Albert (1801-51)
German composer. Moreland tries to distract Maclintick from his depression after Audrey has left with Carolo by asserting that Lortzing's family were "hereditary hangmen for two hundred years" prior to producing him as a composer (*CCR,* 210). Two hundred years may be a bit of an exaggeration. Two of Lortzing's ancestors were hangmen, but they lived in the 17th and 18th centuries. The second of these (Johann Jacob Lortzing) was Albert's great-grandfather who quit his job as hangman to become a gardener and died in

1762. Albert Lortzing's parents were, in fact, both actors, although his father began his professional life as a tanner (combining that with amateur theatricals) and became a professional actor in 1812. Among other works, Lortzing wrote a comic opera called *Casanova*, first performed in 1841. Maclintick recalls this opera after Moreland mentions the composer. This also brings back memories of the years-earlier Casanova / Don Juan debate, causing Maclintick to wonder whether Carolo was of the Casanova or Don Juan type. Moreland thinks he was neither, as Carolo "hasn't the vitality. Too passive" (*CCR*, 210-11). As Jenkins and Moreland leave Maclintick's house on that occasion, Moreland recalls that Barnby had the best answer in the Casanova / Don Juan debate: "One ought to make decisions where women are concerned". But when Jenkins asks him what plans he has (as between Matilda or Priscilla), Moreland replies, "I have none, as usual" (*CCR*, 215).

Lysistrata **
[See MORELAND: Works.]

MACLINTICK *
Habitually grumpy music critic of the "solidly built musical type" (*CCR*, 17-18). Big fan of Moreland, he recognizes the "tidy side" in Moreland's "musical technique" (*CCR*, 5). Speaking of Moreland, he describes himself showing "the proper respect of the poor interpretative hack for the true creative artist" (*CCR*, 19, repeated 215). Displays "severity with Gossage" (*CCR*, 19). Finds Norman Chandler "distasteful". Discusses an Albert Hall concert and the Delius Festival at the Queen's Hall with Gossage (*CCR*, 23).

Working on "a great tome on musical theory which never seems to get finished" (*CCR*, 106). Bookcase "full of composers' biographies and works of musical reference" (*CCR*, 108). Owns a biography of the life of Chabrier (*qv.*) (*CCR*, 109). Finds Shostakovitsch (*qv.*) "Russia's only reputable post-Revolution composer" (*CCR*, 120).

At Mrs Foxe's party for Moreland, finds the latter's new symphony "all right", "respectable", but the reception "just missed being a disaster" (*CCR*, 149). Later suggests angrily to his wife that the music was ",not Moreland's most adventurous' – that the critics had got used to him as an *enfant terrible* and therefore might underestimate the symphony's true value" (*CCR*, 151).

Wife leaves him and he loses job over "rather an astringent article about a concert he was covering" (*CCR*, 204). Drinking hard and working on his book. Met his wife through Gossage (*CCR*, 208). Got his musical tendencies through his mother, who was half Jewish. Discusses Lortzing (*qv.*) with Moreland and Jenkins (*CCR*, 210).

Commits suicide by gassing himself. Tore up the "unreadable book on musical theory" and stopped up the lavatory with it (*SA*, 119). Always liked

Moreland's *Vieux Port* (*SA,* 135). Believed, like Ben Jonson speaking of
human life, that a musician's life remains the same (*BDFR,* 119).

Source. Maclintick is often believed to be modelled partially on the
composer Philip Heseltine (Peter Warlock) (1864-1930), principally because
Heseltine committed suicide by turning on the gas. Other similarities also
exist: Heseltine was a friend of Constant Lambert as Maclintick was of
Moreland; both Heseltine and Maclintick lived in a "very rundown area of
Pimlico"; and both were alcoholics (*Messengers,* 147-49; *CCR,* 106-07).

The Maid of the Mountains
Musical play that opened at Daly's Theatre (*qv.*) on 10 February 1917 and ran
for 1,352 performances. Its female lead was José Collins (1887-1958),
English singer and actress (*qv.*). The show has a comic opera plot set
amongst brigands on the high terrain of southern Europe and involving
Teresa, the "maid of the mountains", and her love for her chief, Baldassare. It
also enjoyed several West End revivals, the most recent in 1972. The book
was by distinguished English playwright Frederick Lonsdale (1881-1954),
who was also the grandfather of Edward Fox (b. 1937), the actor who played
Uncle Giles in the TV film of *Dance.* Lyrics were by poet Harry Graham
(1874-1936), English writer of humorous verse, and music by Harold Fraser-
Simson (1872-1944), British composer of light music. Attended by Ted
Jeavons while on leave in World War I, who considers it a "top-hole show".
It was while attending this performance that Jeavons was given the "glad eye"
by Mildred Haycock, or "as she then was, the Honourable Mildred Blaides"
(*LM,* 175-76).

The Man Who Broke the Bank at Monte Carlo
Music hall song with words and music written by Fred Gilbert (1849-1903) in
1891. He sold the song to British music hall performer Charles Coborn (stage
name of Colin Whitton McCallum 1852-1945) who made it one of his
signature tunes. The song was based on an actual incident in which a
notorious British swindler, Charles de Ville Wells, absconded to Monte Carlo
in the 1890's with ill-gotten gains and had a run of luck at the casino that
broke the bank several times in the process. Gilbert reportedly saw a
newspaper headline poster about "The Man Who Broke the Bank at Monte
Carlo" and thought to himself, there's rhythm in those words, and the rest is
history. The song also inspired a Ronald Coleman movie by the same title
released in 1935 but with a different story line.

Bithel, in his cups, recalls this as one of the songs performed by Sergeant
Ablett as Jenkins and Stringham are trying to lift him from the pavement and
carry him back to his quarters. The recollection causes him to wish the old
music halls could be brought back (*SA,* 181). [See also Divisional Concert.]

MARCELLO, Benedetto (1686-1739)

Italian composer, best known for his church music, particularly *Estro poetico-armonico* (1724-26), a musical setting of the first 50 Psalms. He also wrote several sonatas for one and two ‚cellos which are favored by General Conyers when he isn't playing Gounod's *Ave Maria* (*qv.*) (*LM,* 70). Marcello was by profession a lawyer, occupying several administrative positions in the Venetian Republic, and wrote music as a *"nobile dilletante"*.

Martyrdom of Saint Sebastian

Mediaeval-style mystery play *Le Martyre de St Sébastien* written by Italian poet Gabriele d'Annunzio (1863-1938), first performed in 1911. Incidental music written by Claude Debussy (*qv.*), his first theatrical work since his 1902 opera *Pelléas et Mélisande* (*qv.*). The complete play takes nearly five hours to perform, of which only about one hour consists of Debussy's music. As a consequence, it is seldom performed as a play but rather as a concert piece. Matilda reports that Donners was moved by the performance of dancer, Ida Rubinstein (*qv.*), in a production of this work (*HSH,* 50). Donners must have seen the full production, however, because Rubinstein would not have appeared in the orchestral version. Most likely, he would have seen the performance of the play at Covent Garden in 1931 in which Rubinstein played the lead.

D'Annunzio is said to have been inspired to write a play based on the life of St Sebastian by the sight of Rubinstein's bare legs as he bowed to kiss her feet following her memorable performance in Diaghilev's Russian Ballet (*qv.*) production of the ballet *Schéhérazade*. Donners would, no doubt, have been moved by that background note as well.

The Merry Widow Waltz

From the operetta *The Merry Widow* (*Die lustige Witwe* in German) by Austro-Hungarian composer Franz Lehár (1870-1948), first performed in Vienna in 1905 and in London in 1907. It remains popular to the present day. *The Merry Widow Waltz* from this operetta is identified by Widmerpool as something he had always liked and which made him wish he had "known Vienna in the old days before the war". This is just prior to his receiving a headful of sugar from Barbara Goring (*BM,* 65). The waltz tune is later among the selections from the operetta heard in Venice as they were played by one of the caffè orchestras in the Piazza San Marco while Jenkins and Gwinnett made their way to the Caffè Florian. On that occasion, Jenkins recalls that it was "Widmerpool's favourite waltz" (*TK,* 158). "The Merry Widow Waltz" usually refers to a medley of tunes from two waltzes in the operetta: *The Widows' Waltz* (*Witwenwalzer*) and *Ball Sirens' Waltz* (*Ballsirenwalzer*); it is this medley version that is played in the background when Widmerpool urges Barbara to dance with him in Episode One of the Channel 4 TV film of *Dance*.

The operetta exists in several film and TV versions. Powell seems to have been especially fond of the 1925 film by Erich von Stroheim (1885-1957). Although silent, the film used Lehár's score for musical accompaniment. In his memoirs, Powell recounts his 1954 interview of von Stroheim for *Punch*, and remarks how the director had used the film to combine the operetta's Viennese *belle époque* setting with the equally Viennese subject of Freudian psychoanalysis (the latter represented by von Stroheim's introduction into the plot of a foot-fetish theme). Powell also told von Stroheim how impressed he had been, based on his own war experiences, by the inclusion of a group of "foreign military attachés talking together" in one scene (*Strangers*, 66-71). [See also Anthony Powell, "Stroheim *Redivivus*" (*Punch*, 20 January 1954), 118.]

Messiah
Oratorio by Handel (*qv.*) first performed in 1742 and now one of his most well-known works. It is traditionally performed at Easter and Christmas, and the so-called "Hallelujah Chorus", which occurs at the end of the second of three parts of the work, is so well-known and well-loved that the audience automatically stands at its commencement. This practice is based on the tradition that when King George II (1683-1760, reigned 1727-60) first heard the work, he was so moved that he rose to his feet at this point.

Sillery overhears a boys' choir at practice singing a bit from what he refers to as *"The Messiah"*, although the article is not part of the formal title. This is while on his way to the luncheon arranged by Stringham for Sillery to meet his mother. Sillery remarks that the sound of the "children's voices made me mighty sad". Miss Weedon then notes that Stringham "used to have a nice voice", to which Stringham responds that he might have "earned my living in that way" and to have "especially ... enjoyed singing in the street. Perhaps I shall come to it yet" (*QU*, 214). [See also *WN* 45.]

MEYERBEER, Giacomo (1791-1864)
German-born opera composer. Matilda recommends that Moreland choose *oeufs Meyerbeer* from a restaurant menu, but he as usual dithers, ultimately causing her to put in an order of that dish for him. Her selection may have been made on the basis of the musical association of the dish, although she reminds him that it is one that he always enjoys (*CCR*, 54-55). It consists of shirred (*ie.* baked) or scrambled eggs and lamb kidneys with a truffle sauce. [See also *Anthony Powell Society Newsletter*, **31** (Summer 2008), 21 for recipe and *WN*, 94, mentioning Meyerbeer's opera *Les Huguenots*.]

MIME
One of the dwarfs or Nibelungs in Richard Wagner's opera cycle *The Ring of the Nibelung* (*Der Ring des Nibelungen*) (*qv.*) who appears at the beginning of the third drama of *The Ring* (*ie. Siegfried*). The opera was first performed in

1876 in Bayreuth at Wagner's *Festspielhaus* as part of the first complete performance of *The Ring*.

The curtain rises to reveal Mime "in a state of growing agitation", according to Wagner's stage instructions. The music is written for a tenor voice and is considered by many to be among the most interesting passages Wagner wrote as well as a great challenge for the singer. Mime is desperate for Siegfried (who Mime has raised from a child) to succeed but knows that to do so he must have the one weapon which is indestructible – the sword "Notung" which was previously smashed to pieces against Wotan's shield in the final act of the preceding opera, *The Valkyrie*. It is that sword that Mime is trying to re-forge at the beginning of *Siegfried*.

Also, a nickname applied by Jenkins to an officer of "the Section handling incoming signals". He is described as a "near-midget, middle-aged and two-pipped, with long arms and short legs attached to a squat frame". When Jenkins enters "Mime's" room to secure cables relating to Polish officers leaving the USSR, "it seemed the curtain had just risen on the third drama of *The Ring*" with the wizened lieutenant crouched over an object like Siegfried's sword, interrupted by Jenkins before

> *the burst of guttural tenor notes opened the introductory lament*

> *,Labour unending*
> *Toil without fruit!*
> *The strongest sword*
> *That ever I forged.'*

The sword turns out to be a Sam Browne belt which Lieutenant "Mime" is cleaning (*MP*, 2-3). [See also *WN*, 79.]

When entering the basement of the Section's office building, Jenkins notes that "these murky subterranean regions" might have been thought the proper abode of Mime and his fellow Nibelungs (*MP*, 34); "Mime" is later sighted during an air raid, now promoted to captain (*MP*, 147); General Asbjørnsen's more humble accommodation, originally assigned to Major Prasad, seems to Jenkins to be "an apartment designed for the ablutions of a very thin dwarf, one of Mime's kind" (*MP*, 164); Jenkins wonders whether Captain "Mime" is among those invited to the Victory Thanksgiving Service in St Paul's (*MP*, 218). After the war, at a reunion dinner, Jenkins encounters a member of the MIL unit who also worked in the Section handling incoming telegrams in "an epoch earlier than my own", and who "remembered the stunted middle-aged lieutenant, for ever polishing his Sam Browne belt" (*TK*, 203). The name of the operatic character is usually pronounced the same in English as in German – *ie.* Mee-mah – with the accent on the first syllable. Whether Powell intended to use this pronunciation is difficult to say, but, since he seems to have been familiar with the opera, it appears a likely choice.

The Missouri Waltz
American popular song first published in 1914 based on melody by John V Eppel and arranged by Frederic Knight Logan (1871-1928) with words by JR Shannon, all Americans. It was not particularly popular when originally published, but its survival was assured when it was reported to be the favourite song of US President Harry S Truman (1884-1972, presidential term 1945-53). In 1949, during his presidency, it became the official song of the State of Missouri. Moreland expresses his pleasure when a penny he thrusts into the mechanical piano at the Mortimer produces a raucous rendition of this song (*CCR*, 23).

Molly the Marchioness
Song from musical comedy *A Country Girl* (which ran for over two years at Daly's Theatre (*qv.*) beginning in 1902), music by British critic and composer Lionel Monckton (1861-1924) and words by British lyricist Adrian Ross, pseudonym of Arthur Reed Ropes (1859-1933), who also wrote the lyrics for the English adaptation of *The Merry Widow* (*qv.*). It was also recorded by Flo De Vere on the Gramophone record label. Chips Lovell's father used to hum this song whenever Molly Jeavons' name was mentioned on the premise that she would have continued to be properly addressed by the title of the song if her first husband, Chips' Uncle John, Marquess of Sleaford, hadn't died (*LM*, 17). [See also *WN*, 69 where Dicky Umfraville is proposed as the singer.]

"Monday, Tuesday, Wednesday, Thursday, | May be merry and bright"
Lines from song *I Wish It Was Sunday Night*, recorded in several versions in 1911-12 by Australian-born, British Music Hall entertainer Billy Williams (1878-1915), stage name of Richard Isaac Banks. The song was written in 1911 by Williams in collaboration with Fred Godfrey (1880-1953) and Huntley Trevor. Private Bracey hums it softly, under his breath "when he felt all comparatively right with the world" (*KO*, 21). The Bracey character also sings this song in Episode 2 of the Channel 4 TV film of *Dance*, although unless you are listening very carefully, you might not notice because he is, indeed, reciting it much as described in the novel. It is one of the few songs to survive the transition from novel to film.

MONTEZ, Lola (1821-1861)
Stage name of Irish-born exotic dancer Elizabeth Rosanna Gilbert who was also a courtesan and lover of, *inter alia*, Franz Liszt (*qv.*) and mistress of King Ludwig I of Bavaria (1786-1868, reigned 1825-48), who made her Countess of Landsfield in 1847. She began her dancing career at the age of 16 on the London stage. In the course of an 1855 performance of her Spider Dance in Melbourne, she raised her skirts so high that the audience could see that she

was performing entirely without the benefit of undergarments, causing a considerable scandal in the Australian press. She is also said to be responsible for the expression, "Whatever Lola wants, Lola gets" which became the title of a popular song from the Broadway musical play *Damn Yankees* (1955). Isobel Jenkins refers to Pamela Flitton as "Lola Montez" when she sees her approach Prince Theodoric at the wartime performance of *The Bartered Bride* (*qv.*), no doubt recalling the dancer's liaison with a royal personage as well as her general proclivity to leave a swath of scandal in her wake (*MP,* 101).

In Powell's post-*Dance* novel, *O, How the Wheel Becomes It!* (1983), the writer and protagonist GFH Shadbold is credited with having written a study of Lola Montez and the Bavarian royal family entitled *Bavarian Swan Song,* which is itself an obvious allusion to *Lohengrin* (*qv.*) (*Wheel,* 7).

MORELAND, Hugh **
Twentieth century British composer and conductor.

> *Formed physically in a ,musical' mould, classical in type with a massive, Beethoven-shaped head, high forehead, temples swelling outwards, eyes and nose somehow bunched together in a way to make him glare at times like a High Court judge about to pass sentence. On the other hand, his short, dark, curly hair recalled a dissipated cherub, a less aggressive, more intellectual version of Folly in Bronzino's picture.* (*CCR,* 16)

Biography:
Born within a month or two of Jenkins circa 1905 (*KO,* 82).

Parents died when he was a child, raised by an aunt, whose husband was a musician. Father tubercular, a teacher of music. Lived in Fulham, "juvenile brilliance", poor health. Musical uncle had heard Wagner (*qv.*), Liszt (*qv.*) as a youth, drunk wine with Tchaikovsky (*qv.*) (*CCR,* 4). Also lived with aunt "in rooms at Putney" (*KO,* 83).

Attended Royal College of Music (*KO,* 83). Bachelor flat "in an undistinguished alley on the far side of Oxford Street" (*CCR,* 5).

Marries actress Matilda Wilson (née Betty Updike) circa 1934 (*CCR,* 56). Employment at seaside resort terminated (*CCR,* 104). Daughter born circa 1936, dies shortly afterwards. Lung trouble after baby's death (*CCR,* 129). Lives near Stourwater, where he works on his ballet (*KO,* 89, 94). Matilda leaves him in 1939 (*KO,* 242).

During the war, "a musical job" in Edinburgh (*SA,* 4). An "excess" of employment early in war (*SA,* 93). Begins living with Audrey Maclintick in

1941 (*SA*, 117-18). Tours provinces, from 1942 (*MP*, 35) through 1945 (*MP*, 208).

Conducted *Pelléas et Mélisande* (*qv.*) during "the old Savoy Hill days of the BBC" (*BDFR*, 29). The BBC occupied its Savoy Hill quarters between 1923 and 1932.

By 1958, health has declined, finances worsened, and he lives an "obscure, secluded life" (*TK*, 153). Advises a production of *Die Entführung aus dem Serail* (the *Seraglio*) (*qv.*) for Odo and Rosie Stevens, when he collapses, 1959. Dies in hospital a month or two later (*TK*, 269-77).

Works:
Writes incidental music for Sir Magnus Donners's film version of *Lysistrata* before 1929 (*CCR*, 7, 15; *KO*, 79, 97). Barnby felt it was like "a lot of owls quarrelling in a bicycle factory" (*CCR*, 26).

Works on an opera circa 1934 (*CCR*, 42).

Works on *Music for a Maison de Passe: A Suite* circa 1934 (*CCR*, 42-43).

Symphony, 1936. Works "a long time" on it (*CCR*, 133). "Greeted as a success, but not as an overwhelming success" (*CCR*, 139).

Works on a ballet, 1938 (*KO*, 94).

Tone Poem Vieux Port, composed in Marseilles (*TK*, 270). Heard by General Conyers 1939. "Splendid thing" (*KO*, 211). One of "high spots" in Odo Stevens's early life. Maclintick "always liked" it, according to Audrey (*SA*, 135-36, 150).

Plans *The Fire-watcher's March*, "drums, you know, perhaps triangle and oboe", 1941 (*SA*, 122).

In the late 1950's "one of his recordings [becomes] in a small way a popular hit" (*TK*, 153). (*NB*. This may not be an original composition.)

It is suggested that he write music for a projected but never made film based on a St John Clarke novel and starring Polly Duport (*TK*, 229).

Shortly before his death he jokingly contemplates setting to music the song of *The Dutch Courtezan* from the Jacobean play of that title. [See SPURLING, Books Index.] He considers making it part of an opera on the theme of the legend of *Candaules and Gyges* [see SPURLING, Painting Index], as recently acted out by the Widmerpools, noting that it "would have made Gossage sit up" (*TK*, 269, 276).

Musical Tastes:
Loves mechanical pianos, "fortissimo tunes" of the same period as "*Pale hands I loved beside the Shalimar*" (*qv.*) (1890s) (*CCR*, 2).

The crippled *"Pale hands I loved beside the Shalimar"* singer "unsettled" him; "splendid". [See STREET MUSICIANS (*CCR*, 3).] His aunt used to sing the song, "to the accompaniment of the pianoforte" (*CCR*, 4).

Likes *The Missouri Waltz* (*qv.*) when performed on mechanical piano (*CCR*, 23).

Says he is "no great performer" on the piano (*CCR*, 5-6). Later remarks he could "only do ladylike things such as playing the piano" (*KO*, 98).

Sarcastic about Brahms (*qv.*): "youthful prejudices" (Mr Deacon's words) against the orchestration of Brahms's Second Piano Concerto (*CCR*, 13). Later says he would be willing to "play Brahms's own compositions in a brothel, part of the *Requiem* would be very suitable" (*SA*, 134).

Interest in Chabrier (*qv.*) (*CCR*, 109 ff; *Messengers*, 60).

"Said to be good at controlling an orchestra" (*CCR*, 214).

Favourite "pirate-like man" with wooden leg who fiddled off Piccadilly Circus and was "inclined to play Saint-Saëns" (*SA*, 6). Sees him behind the London Pavilion playing *Softly Awakes My Heart* in 1941 (*SA*, 114). [See STREET MUSICIANS: One-eyed peg-leg fiddle player.]

Would only have "partially approved" of music at Victory Thanksgiving Service: "Welsh Guards strummed away at Holst, Elgar, Grieg, finally, Handel's „Water Music'" (*qv.*) (*MP*, 218).

Walton's (*qv.*) "Grand March" was "in Moreland's line" (*MP*, 227).

Musical Philosophy:
A "precise, tidy side" "mirrored in his music" (*CCR*, 5).

> *Whatever the critics say, good or bad, all works of art must go through a maturing process before taking their allotted place in the scheme of things.* (*CCR*, 139)

Also he

> *possessed his healthy share of liking to startle, in spite of his own innate antagonism to professional startlers.* (*CCR*, 139-40)

Asks is it better to write a symphony for oneself or a comic song? Or a poor imitation of Stravinsky?

> *"Is art action, an alternative to action, the enemy of action, or nothing whatever to do with action?"* (*KO*, 76)

*"The arts derive entirely from taking decisions ... That is why they
make such unspeakably burdensome demands on all who practice
them."* (*KO*, 80)

*"The abominable question of musical interpretation eternally
bedevils a composer's life."* (*KO*, 76)

A musical opinion of Anne Stepney Umfraville outrages Moreland, "an easy
enough thing to do" (*KO*, 118).

[See also Existential Music; Russian Ballet; SCRIABIN.]

Source:
Moreland is modelled generally, though not specifically, on Powell's friend,
the composer / conductor Constant Lambert (1905-51). Powell wrote
(*Messengers*, 60):

*If I have been skilful enough, lucky enough, to pass on any echo of
Lambert's incomparable wit, then Moreland is like him; in other
respects the things that happen to Moreland approximate to the
things that happened to Lambert only within the extent that all
composers' lives have something in common.*

MOZART, Wolfgang Amadeus (1756-91)
Austrian composer of over 600 works, including 22 operas. Among the
operas are *Die Entführung aus dem Serail* (*qv.*), *Idomeneo* (*qv.*) and *Don
Giovanni.* [See *Don Juan.*]

Mozart also figures in an interesting anecdote recounted by Powell in his
memoirs. Lambert and his wife were weekend guests with Powell and
Wyndham Lloyd, a scientist, at Woodgate, the home of Gerald Reitlinger. In
the course of a session of planchette, the pencil refused to write at first, due
perhaps to Lloyd's scientific skepticism. After the others retired to different
pursuits, Powell and Reitlinger continued to rest their fingers on the board
without much hope of activity when "a long sloping 18th century hand
announced itself as Mozart". Lambert was recalled to test the presence and
asked who was his favourite mistress, when and where did his affair with her
take place and what did she look like. The answers given are recorded in the
memoirs but were later found to be unverifiable except for the fact that the
composer was not in Naples, the location given by the presence as the scene
of his affair, at the time he said it took place (*Messengers,* 176-77).

Another Mozart-related reference occurs in Powell's last novel *The Fisher
King* (1986). This is described in Nicholas Birns, *Understanding Anthony
Powell* (Columbia, SC, 2004), 264:

*there are two Americans, obviously, though never specifically
revealed, a homosexual couple. Called by their t-shirts, "Basically*

Bach" and "Marginally Mahler" (inspired by a Mostly Mozart t-shirt Powell saw on an actual cruise, presumably without knowing this referred to a festival), they engaged in musical discussions. These are probably lineal, if attenuated, descendants of those Gossage, Moreland, and Maclintick would have undertaken at a certain restaurant. "More than once Lamont caught the name of Boulez". (Fisher, 50)

[See also *J82-86*, 220.] The reference in the quote is to Pierre Boulez (b. 1925), French composer of modernist classical music and conductor of, *inter alia,* the BBC Symphony Orchestra (1971-75).

La Muette de Portici
[See AUBER.]

MUSIC LOVERS, AMATEUR PERFORMERS, PATRONS AND OTHERS EXHIBITING MUSICAL ATTITUDES

<u>Ablett, Sergeant</u> ** Known for his star turn of singing, dancing and comedy at Divisional Concerts (*SA*, 217, 219); has sung *The Man who broke the Bank at Monte Carlo* (*SA*, 181).

<u>Andriadis, Milly</u> ** Said by Moreland to be trying to help Carolo out of financial difficulties by "arranging a performance in her house or something" (*CCR*, 25). [See also *WN*, 82.]

<u>Bithel, Lieutenant "Bith"</u> ** Territorial lieutenant who sings drunkenly "A song of love" and dances when ragged (*VB*, 27); acts successfully as producer-director of Divisional Concert (*SA*, 9); while drunk, sings "Fol-low, fol-low, we will fol-low Davies" "in a thin piping voice, not unlike Max Pilgrim's" (*SA*, 180); while at Fiona Cutt's wedding, a member of Murtlock's cult, sings "Open now the crystal fountain" (*HSH*, 216); later, "From every dark nook they press forward to meet me" (*HSH*, 219) finally, "When I tread the verge of Jordan" (*HSH*, 238); after he consigns Stringham's Modigliani drawing to Barnabas Henderson, he sings "Fol-low, fol-low, we will fol-low Gwatkin" (*HSH*, 265).

<u>Brandreth, Dr</u> ** School friend of Jenkins who is also a Wagner fan and expert on the medical conditions of famous musicians (*CCR*, 101,104-05).

<u>Bruylant</u> ** Belgian attaché who replaces Kucherman; has musical leanings, but less pronounced than Colonel Hlava's; beats time almost imperceptibly with his finger to music of Welsh Guards (*MP*, 215, 218).

<u>Clark, St John</u> ** Novelist who also "expressed himself with equal force regarding painting and music. He had certainly been associated with opposition to the Post-Impressionists in 1910; also in leading some minor skirmish in operatic circles soon after the Armistice" (*AW*, 20).

Conyers, General Aylmer ** Amateur cellist, who always practices "until five o'clock" when he is in London; plays *Ave Maria* by Gounod, also pieces by Saint-Saëns and Marcello's sonatas:

> *A low melancholy wailing ... notes of a hidden orchestra,*
> *mysterious, even a shade unearthly, as if somewhere in the vicinity*
> *gnomes were thumbing strange instruments in a cave.*

Admires Moreland's *Tone Poem Vieux Port.* Meets his second wife, Tuffy Weedon, at a concert (*LM*, 69-73; *KO*, 39, 208, 211, 218; *SA*, 6).

Dempster ** Plays piano "rather notably", sometimes in duets with Colonel Hlava (*MP*, 24).

Donners, Sir Magnus Aside from his industrial activities, a patron of painting and music; commissions Moreland to write incidental music for a film, *Lysistrata*; enjoys orchestral, operatic and dance performances; listens only to best music during a two-month cultural development period when a young man; and in old age listens to gramophone recordings of his favourites, including *Parsifal,* which Matilda plays for him, and "sheds tears over the sufferings of the Chinese slave girl in *Turandot,* no less when watching Ida Rubinstein in *The Martyrdom of St Sebastian*" (*CCR*, 15; *KO*, 79, 92-93, 97; *TK*, 270-71; *HSH*, 50).

Duport, Jean Said by her husband Bob to lack any musical knowledge, but see CHALIAPIN.

Duport, Robert Despite his outward appearance of a commercial orientation, has surprisingly deep interest in music and painting; always liked music; not all that keen on Auber, but has heard *La Muette de Portici* several times (*VB*, 124-25; *MP*, 190; *HSH*, 252, 257).

Foxe, Amy ** Patroness of Moreland, who – as a consequence of her enigmatic relationship with Norman Chandler – gives a party around the time of the Abdication (December 1936) for Moreland's symphony (*CCR*, 133-34, 140, 147).

Gittens, Lance-Corporal Gareth ** Member of Jenkins' Welsh company who sings a verse of *Cwm Rhondda* to himself while sorting "huge piles of Army Form ,ten-ninety-eight'" (*VB*, 102).

Gwylt, Corporal Ivor ** Member of Jenkins' Welsh company who sings *Arm-in- arm together* to the barmaid Maureen, much to the distress of Captain Gwatkin (*VB*, 228-29).

Hlava, Colonel ** Keen on music; fond of Czech composers; plays piano, but not "quite in Dempster's class"; sometimes plays a duet with Dempster;

hosts Jenkins and Isobel at a performance of *The Bartered Bride* (*MP*, 24, 96-8, 101).

Huntercombe, Lady (Sybil) ** Thought by Mrs Foxe to have been the "Lady Sybil" mentioned in a "funny" song by Max Pilgrim; takes a keen interest in music and criticizes the choir at Stringham's wedding for singing "dreadfully sharp ... It set my teeth on edge" (*CCR*, 51, 143-44).

Huntercombe, Lord (Walter) ** More concerned with painting than with music but, although not musically inclined, serves on board that sponsors performance of *The Bartered Bride* and invites Prince Theodoric to accompany him (*CCR*, 143; *MP*, 98).

Jeavons, Ted ** Nice baritone; favours old music hall and WWI-era songs; doesn't like contemporary popular music (*LM*, 186; *KO*, 235, 253-54; *BDFR*, 2); his head sometimes seethed "with forgotten melodies, for ever stirring him to indiscretion by provoking memories of an enchanted past" (*LM*, 218); at Dicky Umfraville's club, sings in "an unexpectedly deep and attractive voice", "If you were the only – girl in the world" (*LM*, 177-8); later that night sings "He ran a pin | In Gwendolyn" (*LM*, 201); at one of Lady Molly's parties sings "I'm a trooper, I'm a trooper" (*KO*, 239); after Erridge's funeral sings "When Father went down to Southend" (*BDFR*, 90-1).

Jones, D ** One of the orderlies in Jenkins's Welsh company who sings *South of the Border*; presumably he was the soloist: "a man's voice, deep throated and penetrating ... in a lament of heart-breaking melancholy" (*VB*, 4, 6-7).

Manasch, Sir Herbert and Lady, parents of Rosie ** Patrons of musical events; once sponsored a charity concert in their house at which Moreland conducted (*CCR*, 177; *BDFR*, 100).

Murtlock, Leslie "Scorpio" ** Choirboy in his youth; sang "delightfully" for Cannon Fenneau's parish church the hymn *Hail Gladdening Light*, and won a scholarship to a choir school (*HSH*, 131-32).

Pontner ** Translator and small time dealer in paintings and drawings who is "musically inclined in a manner Moreland could approve, a qualification by no means common" (*TK*, 67).

Promising pianist ** Young girl, known to Moreland's aunt, who was said to have promising talents as a pianist; Moreland, before his Royal College of Music days, was "impressed by the idea of a female pianist who was promising"; she fell into the clutches of Dr Trelawney and committed suicide by throwing herself off a mountain in Wales (*KO*, 83-84).

Short, Sir Leonard ** A "civil servant with musical leanings" who used to frequent the elder Manaschs' musical events and attends *Seraglio* (*qv.*) with the Widmerpools (*TK*, 232).

Stanley ** Audrey Maclintick's brother; friend of Gossage; favours Sibelius; "all the music in the family went into Stanley" (*CCR*, 208-10).

Stepney, Peggy ** Said by her first husband, Charles Stringham, to be not musical; "Music did not run in the family. Mountfichet [the family estate] was not a house to stimulate music. You might compose a few dirges there, I suppose" (*CCR*, 175).

Stevens, Odo ** Fan of Moreland's: "Hearing your *Tone Poem Vieux Port* was one of the high spots of my early life"; also a fan of Max Pilgrim; with his wife, Rosie, hosts performance of *Die Entführung aus dem Serail* (the *Seraglio* (*qv.*)), advised but not conducted by Moreland (*SA*, 134-36, 145; *TK*, 224-29).

Stevens, Rosie Manasch ** Second generation patroness, hosts charitable performance of *Seraglio* (*qv.*) advised but not conducted by Moreland (*TK*, 224-29).

Stringham, Charles ** Argues that one of the Dolly Sisters is the mother of the other (*QU*, 38); attends the Russian Ballet (*QU*, 56); used to have a nice voice: "I really might have earned my living that way ... I should especially have enjoyed singing in the street" (*QU*, 214); quotes hymn ("Not for ever by still waters") (*CCR* 183); hums "a bar or two of a jerky tune: ‚So-let-each-cavalier-who-loves-honour-and-me'" (*qv.*) (*SA*, 81); misses chance to debut as vocalist at Divisional Concert when Mobile Laundry Unit is posted to Far East (*SA*, 223-24); fond of hymns, "addicted to quoting their imagery within the context of his own life" (*MP*, 221-22).

Tolland, Priscilla ** Works for "the organisation raising money for the promotion of opera" which brings her in touch to some degree with the musical world in which she is otherwise not much interested; she leaves that job after breaking up with Moreland; is given a brooch, probably by Moreland, with a musical motif – mandolin with musical symbols on either side – which Odo Stevens offers to have repaired when they first meet (*CCR*, 137; 225; *VB*, 143).

Tolland, Robert ** A "keen concert-goer and a frequenter of musical parties"; on the Board of an organisation for the promotion of opera and thinks he can help Priscilla, his sister, secure a job there; plays Debussy's *Iberia* on the gramophone, loves movement entitled *Parfums de la Nuit* (*CCR*, 61-3; 70; 137).

Trapnel, X ** Author who likes to recall high spots in silent films emphasized by "several seconds of monotonous music rising louder and louder, until, almost deafening, the notes suddenly jar out of tune in a frightful discord: the train is derailed; the canoe swept over the rapids; the knife plunged into the naked flesh. All is over. The action is cut: calm music again, perhaps no music at all" (*BDFR,* 162).

Walpole-Wilson, Sir Gavin ** Fond of Slezak, heard him "many a time and oft" perform *Lohengrin* (*BM,* 35).

Widmerpool, Mrs ** Tells Moreland that Scriabin's *Poème de l'extase* is her "favourite musical work" (*KO,* 242).

Widmerpool, Kenneth ** Fond of waltzes, particularly *The Merry Widow Waltz*; his dance style described as "ploughing his way round the room, as if rowing a dinghy in rough water"; shows little interest in Moreland's music, recalling – when introduced to him a second time – only that he plays the piano; when first sighted in his military uniform, he "had almost the air of being about to perform a music hall turn, sing a patriotic song or burlesque, with ‚patter', an army officer" (*BM,* 60, 65; *KO,* 134; *TK,* 158).

Williams, Private WH ** Orderly in Jenkins' Welsh company, who joins Jones, D, in singing *South of the Border* (*VB,* 4-7).

My Heart Stood Still
Song with words by Lorenz Hart (1895-1943) and music by Richard Rodgers (1903-1979). Both born in New York City, they wrote nearly thirty Broadway musicals. There are several stories associated with the composition of this song. The idea is said to have occurred to them when a crash between two Paris taxis was narrowly averted and one of the female passengers in their cab exclaimed: "Oh, my heart stood still!" Hart immediately responded, "Say, that's a good name for a song", and Rodgers (wondering how Hart could think of business at such a juncture) wrote it down in his address book. Later, in London, Rodgers came across the words and wrote out a tune. When Hart joined him, he added some lyrics, which are remarkable because they contain only six two-syllable words, the rest being of one syllable.

This song was first used in the 1927 West End revue *One Dam Thing After Another* produced by English impresario CB Cochran (*qv.*). Subsequent to Cochran's revue, the Rodgers and Hart song was also used in two Broadway runs of their musical comedy *A Connecticut Yankee* (1927 and 1943) which was based on Mark Twain's novel. In Powell's novel, on the "Night of the Three Parties", the song is performed first by a dance band at the Huntercombes' ball (*BM,* 58) and later at Mrs Andriadis' party by a

> *hunch-back wearing a velvet smoking-jacket ... playing an*
> *accordion, writhing backwards and forwards as he attacked his*
> *instrument with demiurgic frenzy.* (*BM*, 105, 139)

In the Channel 4 TV film of *Dance*, this song is used in Episode One as dance music, as in the novel, but the accordionist, who plays at Mrs Andriadis' party, lacks a hunchback in the film and plays two different tunes – *La Paloma* and "*I Get Ideas*". The song also provides the title music for Episode Two of the film and is used as background music in both Episodes Two and Four.

"My lips smile no more, my heart loses its lightness" (*The Ash Grove*)
Beginning of the final verse of a Welsh folk song which is sung sombrely by the Battalion as it forms up on arrival at the "small, unalluring industrial town" where it is to be stationed in Northern Ireland (*VB*, 45-46). The song is heard again as Widmerpool and other members of the Murtlock cult are considering whether to accept an *ad hoc* invitation to the Akworth-Cutts wedding reception. On this occasion, it is Bithel who breaks out with the last four lines of this song, contributing to Widmerpool's decision to accept the invitation (*HSH*, 219). On both occasions, the words are from the final verse of the English version written by English dramatist John Oxenford (1812-77) who was also something of a linguist. [See also *WN*, 158.]

New Hungarian String Quartet
Music group formed in 1937 and led by Zoltán Székely (1903-2001), a student of Zoltán Kodály (1882-1967) and closely associated with Béla Bartók (1881-1945), both Hungarian composers. Donners asks Moreland whether he has heard this group perform, although Donners says he himself has not. Perhaps, because the group had been formed only shortly before Donners asks this question in 1938, he refers to it as the "New Hungarian String Quartet" (*KO*, 116).

NIJINSKY, Vaslav (1890-1950)
Russian ballet dancer and choreographer, born in Kiev, Ukraine, to a Russified Polish family. He became the male lead of Diaghilev's Russian Ballet company (*qv.*) when it performed in Paris in 1909. He is considered one of the foremost male ballet dancers of the 20th Century. [See also "*L'Après-midi d'un faune*" (*CCR*, 49).]

"Not for ever by still waters | Would we idly rest and stay"
Words from the American Unitarian hymn *Father, Hear the Prayer We Offer*, words by Mrs Love Maria Willis (1824-1908), the wife of an American physician from Rochester, NY, generally sung to the tune *Sussex*, an adaptation of a traditional English folk tune by English composer Ralph Vaughan Williams (1872-1958).

Stringham is reminded of the words of the hymn and recites them in response to Miss Weedon's efforts to forestall his plans to escort Audrey Maclintick to a night club following his mother's party in honour of the premiere of Moreland's symphony. Miss Weedon offers both Stringham and Audrey a lift home, but Stringham cites the hymn as support for avoiding such a "life of ease" and taking "the hard road". In the end, Miss Weedon prevails (*CCR,* 183-85).

Now Thank We All Our God
Hymn sung at the Victory Thanksgiving Service which Jenkins thinks to be "of German origin", correctly as it turns out. The original words (*Nun danket alle Gott*) are by Martin Rinkart (1586-1649) and the music possibly by him but sometimes attributed to Johan Crüger (1598-1662), with harmony arranged later by Felix Mendelssohn (1809-47), all German. Jenkins thinks whoever was responsible for choice of this hymn has "either forgotten" its German origin "or judged it peculiarly apposite" (*MP,* 225). The English translation of the hymn as sung at the Thanksgiving Service was by Catherine Winkworth (1829-78), English hymn writer and educator, who also translated numerous other German hymns into English versions that are still widely used.

"Now we are come to the sun's hour of rest"
Lines from the hymn *Hail, Gladdening Light*, words translated from the Greek original *Phos Hilarion* by John Keble (1792-1866), English cleric and leader of the Oxford Movement for whom Keble College, Oxford is named. Performed as a solo "so delightfully" by Scorpio (then Leslie) Murtlock as a choirboy at Canon Fenneau's South London parish church. Fenneau recounts the difficulty he had persuading Murtlock's parents (who belonged to a small fanatical religious sect) to allow him to join the choir. "I should never have done so, had Leslie himself not insisted on joining. His will was stronger than theirs" (*HSH,* 131-32).

It is sung to various tunes but the one most likely in use during Scorpio's choirboy days (and the one most likely to have been sung as a solo) would probably be *Sebaste* by John Stainer (1840-1901), English composer and organist. Today, it is usually sung in an arrangement by Irish composer Charles Wood (1866-1926) as an eight-part, double choir anthem, which cannot be performed as a solo.

"on my own-io"
Stringham recalls this phrase from an Edwardian song as he enlists help from Nick Jenkins in returning the drunken Bithel to his sleeping quarters (*SA,* 177). The song is *"Oh! Oh! Antonio",* recorded in 1908 by Australian music hall singer Florrie Forde, stage name of Florence Mary Flannagan (1876-1940). She also popularized and recorded many other songs of the WWI era,

including "*Pack Up Your Troubles in Your Old Kit Bag*" and "*It's a Long Way to Tipperary*". The song was written by Clarence Wainwright Murphy and Dan Lipton and published in 1908. It is about an Italian ice cream vendor, and the words of the chorus go like this:

> *Oh! Oh! Antonio, he's gone away*
> *Left me alone-io, all on my own-io.*
> *I want to meet him with his new sweetheart*
> *Then up will go Antonio and his ice cream cart.*

Leopold Bloom also recalls the words of this song on two occasions in James Joyce's (1882-1941) *Ulysses* (1922), but he remembers them somewhat differently from the song as published:

> *As bad as old Antonio*
> *For he left me on my ownio.*

[See James Joyce, *Ulysses* (Modern Library, New York, 1934), 96, 616.]

Powell knew the song as a child during the period when it was popular and recalled that during the Edwardian period there was an "affectation of Italianizing words" (*Infants,* 50). He may also have known the song (or been reminded of it) from Joyce's novel.

"*Open now the crystal fountain*"
[See *Guide Me O Thou Great Jehovah.*]

"*oranges and lemons | bells of St Clement's*"
Opening lines from traditional English nursery rhyme that is sung as part of a playground game. The rhyme is sung to a tune that mimics the sounds of a peal of English church-bells:

> *Orange and lemons*
> *Say the bells of St Clement's*

Several other churches are mentioned in the course of the rhyme, all in the City of London. St Clement's refers to the Church of St Clement, Eastcheap, on Clement Lane, EC4 (not St Clement Dane, another City church, as is sometimes claimed). St Clement, Eastcheap, was at one time, when the Thames was wider, near the wharf where citrus fruit was landed from the Mediterranean. It is said that the bells of St Clement, Eastcheap, pealed when such a cargo arrived. References to the rhyme are recorded as early as 1744 but the "Oranges and Lemons" line did not appear until 1858. Borrit, "as always making a joke", recites the rhyme when announcing to Jenkins his intention to return to his family firm of wholesale fruit dealers (*MP,* 198). In the pre-war novel *Agents and Patients* (1936) two of the characters, while visiting Berlin, watch as two groups of Nazis, "coming from opposite directions, passed each other and saluted, as if about to initiate a game of oranges and lemons" (*A&P,* 145).

"Pale hands I loved beside the Shalimar" (Kashmiri Song)

This is the first line of *Kashmiri Song,* an Edwardian love song with Indian theme; music by Amy Woodforde-Finden (1860-1919) and words by Laurence Hope (pseudonym for Adela Florence Nicolson, née Cary) (1865-1904). The song was first published in *Four Indian Love Lyrics from the Garden of Kama* (1902), although the poem itself had been previously published separately, in England as *The Garden of Kama* (1901) and in the US as *India's Love Lyrics* (1902). *Kashmiri Song* achieved considerable popularity in the Edwardian period, perhaps not least because of the scandal arising from the revelation that the lyricist Laurence Hope was in real life Adela Florence Nicolson, the wife of an Indian Army officer. The song remained popular until World War II, although Jenkins and Moreland would have found it dated by then. It is thought that the two women who wrote the words and music never met. Shalimar could refer to one of two Shalimar Gardens, one in Kashmir, as would be suggested by the song's title, or the other in Lahore, where the lyricist lived with her Army officer husband. "Pale hands" would also favour Kashmir where those native to the area have noticeably paler skins than would be the case in Lahore.

Kashmiri Song is first encountered by Jenkins and Moreland being sung by the "blonde woman on crutches" in Gerrard Street, Soho at the beginning of *CCR.* [See STREET MUSICIANS: Crippled blonde woman.] Jenkins and Moreland "afterwards discussed the whereabouts of the Shalimar, and why the locality should have been the haunt of pale hands and those addicted to them". Such locales as a nightclub, "bordel" or an establishment catering for exotic tastes are suggested. Moreland remarks that the woman's singing has "unsettled" him.

> *"What nostalgia. It was really splendid. "Whom do you lead on Rapture's roadway far?" What a pertinent question. But where can we go?"*

The answer by Jenkins is "tea at Casanova's Chinese Restaurant ... suitably oriental after the song" (*CCR,* 1-3).

Still in the street, Moreland, as was his habit, continues with the subject of the song, although Jenkins thinks it another "trivial matter less amusing to others than to himself". Moreland wonders whether the song is set on a boat, since "houseboats are a feature of Kashmir", which is in the title. He also recalls that his aunt in Fulham used to sing the song "to the accompaniment of the pianoforte". He then sings a version himself while still in the street "as loudly trilled by his aunt" but with commentary as to how that contrasted to the rendering by the crippled blonde woman. Jenkins opines that it might have been set on "a houseboat of ill-fame", which Moreland finds an "enjoyable idea" and is overwhelmed by the desire "for something of the sort ... this afternoon". In the end, they reject both the bordello and Casanova's Chinese Restaurant in favour of "the adventitious vintages of Shaftesbury Avenue" (*CCR,* 3-5).

Jenkins is later reminded of the song in connection with Lord Warminster who died in Kashmir. His visits were, however, not made

> *on account of the sensual attractions extolled in the Kashmiri Love Song [sic] but for pleasure in the more general beauty of its valleys, and the shooting of ibex there. (CCR,* 58)

The song has been recorded several times, perhaps most notably by film actor Rudolph Valentino (1895-1926), his only recording as a singer, who recorded it for Brunswick Records in 1923, with the release delayed until 1926, after his death. It was also used as incidental music for Valentino's 1921 silent film *The Sheik.*

At least two writers whose work Powell admired have also used this song to comic effect. In Evelyn Waugh's *The Loved One* (1948) the hero overhears music described as "The Hindu Love-song" playing at two different locations in Whispering Glades cemetery (Evelyn Waugh, *The Loved One* (Penguin, 1951) 35, 36). Two Waugh scholars agree that he must be referring to the *Kashmiri Song,* although in Waugh's related essay about the cemetery on which Whispering Glades was based, the editors of the US version (which appeared in *Life* magazine) changed the name of the song to "Indian Love Call," while the British version appearing in the *Tablet* preserved the name used in the novel and as written by Waugh in the essay (Paul A Doyle, *Reader's Companion to Works of Evelyn Waugh* (1988), 62). The narrator of Barbara Pym's *Glass of Blessings* (1958) recalls that the hand of a fellow Wren officer being held in Italy by her lover during the WWII occupation was "soft and smooth, delicately pink-tipped, like those in Laurence Hope's *Indian Love Lyrics* which my mother used to sing in Amy Woodforde Finden's settings" (42).

More recently, the song (or at least the first few lines) was used to comic effect in the 1970s ITV comedy series *Rising Damp;* in the Series 3 episode entitled "Fawcett's Python" (transmitted 10 May 1977), Miss Jones plays the recorder in accompaniment of the curate whose attempt to sing the song is interrupted by the snake of the title. The song and the crippled blonde singer appear briefly in Episode 2 of the Channel 4 TV film. In the film, she is singing on the street in front of a pub as Jenkins leaves after having met with Jean Duport. This scene has no direct counterpart in the novel but occurs chronologically at roughly the time Jenkins and Moreland heard the singer in 1933.

Les parfums de la nuit
[See *Iberia.*]

Parsifal

Mystery play ("*Bühnenweihfestspiel*") by Richard Wagner (*qv.*) first performed in Bayreuth in 1882. The story involves the quest of a mediaeval knight for the spear used to pierce Christ during the Crucifixion and is based on Wolfram von Eschenbach's 13th century epic *Parzival*, which in turn borrows elements of its plot from Chrestien de Troyes' 12th century romance *Perceval, le Conte du Graal* (*Perceval, the Story of the Grail*). Wagner's theme is the spiritual quest of his hero – a pure simpleton – for redemption by abstention from questions, reasoning, explanations *etc.* to achieve "pure being" in charity and piety. It is one of Sir Magnus Donners' favourites, which, according to Norman Chandler, Matilda played for him on the gramophone in his declining years (*HSH,* 50).

Parsifal also plays a pivotal role in the myth of the Fisher King which is a key to the plot and theme of Powell's last novel and provides its title. In that novel, he is referred to as Perceval, with a cross reference to the Germanic version, Parzival (although Wagner changed the spelling for his version to "Parsifal" which is a pun on "*Fal Parsi*", the pure simpleton.). [See *FK,* Chapter 3; see also *J82-86,* 243 where Powell relates a discussion of this point with his dentist.]

Pavilion (Brighton)

Most likely, this refers to what is now called the Dome Concert Hall, located in the grounds of the Royal Pavilion in Brighton. The building was constructed in 1805 as the riding stables for the Prince Regent, later George IV (1762-1830, reigned 1820-30), who used the Royal Pavilion as one of his residences. In 1866 the riding stables were converted into a concert hall and, after two subsequent restorations, the restored building continues to serve that purpose. The concert hall can seat up to 1,872 persons. Jenkins believes that his parents were introduced to Mr Deacon while attending a concert at this venue (*BM,* 5; *KO,* 80). His parents lived in Brighton prior to moving to Stonehurst before WWI, and Mr Deacon lived there prior to moving to Paris after WWI.

In his memoirs, Powell says that, before her marriage, his mother, living in Brighton at the time,

> *without any profound feeling for music, was at the same time skilled*
> *enough at the banjo, then all the rage, to get laudatory notices*
> *when she gave amateur performances at the Pavilion.* (*Infants,* 27)

A picture of his mother holding the banjo is included in *Infants,* plate 10a.

PAVLOVA, Anna (1881-1931)
[See Russian Ballet.]

Pelléas et Mélisande
Most likely a reference to the 1902 opera by French composer Claude
Debussy (*qv.*), his only completed opera. The libretto of the opera is based on
the text of the play of the same name by the Belgian poet and playwright
Maurice Maeterlinck (1862-1949). The theme is the doomed, forbidden love
of the title characters. The project was first proposed by Debussy to
Maeterlinck in 1891 and renewed in 1893 at which point the latter agreed. In
the decade of the opera's gestation, Debussy's life reportedly mirrored the
drama and tragedy of the three-way love affair of the opera. Moreover, when
the production was finally in rehearsal, Maeterlinck and Debussy fell out over
the latter's refusal to cast the former's mistress as Mélisande. Moreland
conducted a work of this title prior to an "all but disastrous incident"
involving Bagshaw on the top of a London bus (*BDFR,* 29). Other
possibilities are orchestral works by Arnold Schönberg, Gabriel Fauré or Jean
Sibelius also related to Maeterlinck's play, but these would have been offered
as individual pieces in a performance that included other works, rather than
taking up an entire performance, as would Debussy's opera. [See also
Martyrdom of Saint Sebastian.]

PILGRIM, Max **
Singer and pianist, performing cabaret acts. Appears at Milly Andriadis'
party, singing in "a tremulous, quavering voice, like that of an immensely
ancient lady". His song, *Tess of Le Touquet* (*qv.*), angers Mr Deacon, who
eventually gets into a "frantic quarrel" with him (*BM,* 114-5, 118, 120, 148-
9). Mrs Foxe is reminded of his song beginning "I want to dazzle Lady
Sybil" when Norman Chandler tells her that he has invited Max to a post-
performance dinner; she wonders if "he meant it to be about Sybil
Huntercombe, do you think? It's so like her" (*CCR,* 51). Performs "*Di, Di, in
her collar and tie*" (*qv.*) at Dicky Umfraville's club (*LM,* 185-86). During the
war does a revival at the Café de Madrid (*qv.*) with such songs as *Tess of Le
Touquet; Heather, Heather, she's under the weather.* Has been with ENSA
(*qv.*) entertaining the forces (*SA,* 115-6). [See also *WN,* 82.] At the Madrid,
expressing "to audiences all that was most nostalgic", he is interrupted by the
blitz: "It was getting the bird in a big way" (*SA,* 154-5).

In his memoirs Powell recalls performances of Douglas Byng (1893-1987),
British comic singer of revue and cabaret, who performed "with ineffable
sparkle ... his own songs for the piano, to what was usually a conventionally
smart world" at the Café de Paris, which was the inspiration for the fictional
Café de Madrid (*Faces,* 51). Byng shares many characteristics with Max
Pilgrim.

Le Poème de l'extase
[See SCRIABIN.]

Popes and Music
In his discussion of musical censorship by the Soviets, Moreland is reminded of "a period in the Middle Ages when the Pope forbade certain chords under pain of excommunication" (*CCR*, 120). Here, he may be referring to a 1328 Papal Bull issued by Pope John XXII (1249-1334, né Jacques Duèze, Papacy 1316-34) complaining about "new methods" of singing and composition, especially concerning descants and the use of popular (and often profane) songs underpinning the polyphony. He felt that such music caused

> *devotion, the true aim of all worship, [to be] neglected and*
> *wantonness, which is to be shunned, [to be] increased. We hasten*
> *to forbid these methods.*

Another possible source of Moreland's reference might be an earlier dispute over the introduction of the "tritone" into ecclesiastical music. The Benedictine monk, Guido of Arezzo (991/2-1033) used this restless interval or dissonant and slightly unsettling chord, to help monastic singers remember Gregorian chants. His success in training the singers at the Pomposa Abbey, near Ferrara, spread throughout northern Italy, and caused such hostility among the elders of that institution that Guido moved to Arezzo, where there were no abbeys, to continue his work. The use of the "tritone", which later came to be known as "*diabolus in musica*", while contributing to Guido's banishment from Pomposa, does not seem to have been the cause of anything as serious as excommunication. Indeed, Pope John XIX (d. 1032, né Romanus, Papacy 1024-32) was so pleased with Guido's later work in Arezzo, that he invited him to Rome in 1028.

It is also possible that Moreland is thinking of a dispute between the Italian composer Giovanni Pierluigi da Palestrina (1525/26-1594) and Pope Paul IV (1476-1559, né Giovanni Pietro Carafa, Papacy 1555-59). While no one was threatened with excommunication on this occasion either, which took place during the Renaissance, not the Middle Ages, Palestrina was, in fact, rebuked by Paul IV through loss of his position in the Sistine Chapel choir. But this seems to have been due to the fact that Palestrina was married while holding an appointment limited to one in Holy Orders rather than to any attempts on his part to influence liturgical music reforms with which Paul IV was not in agreement. Palestrina's posthumous reputation led to his being seen as the "saviour of sacred music" from the policies laid down by the Council of Trent (1545-63). These policies prescribed, *inter alia*, that the clarity of the words in liturgical music not be obscured by the music itself. While Palestrina's work (such as the *Missa Papae Marcelli*) represents a successful implementation of this policy without compromising the polyphony he advocated, his reputation as "saviour of sacred music" probably owes more to his romantic image as reflected in 19th Century scholarship, most notably in his biography by Giuseppe Baini (1775-1844), than to any crusading efforts on his part during in his lifetime. This same image was adopted by the German composer Hans Pfitzner (1869-1949) in his opera (or "musical legend") *Palestrina*, first performed in 1917.

Moreland, as a graduate of the Royal College of Music, would certainly be aware of these historical musical controversies involving various Popes and composers. However, to know which one he is referring to in his somewhat offhand remark is something about which readers can only speculate. He may, indeed, be referring to a combination of various elements of these incidents based on his memory at the time he makes the remark in question.

The Popular Song from Lilliburlero to Lili Marlene **

One of the books that Hugh Moreland suggests he might write (but never does) as an alternative to his music which he felt was under-appreciated (*BDFR,* 120).

Lilliburlero (or *Lillibullero*) is a 17th century satirical ballad long associated with the Protestant (Orange) cause in Ireland. The original words are generally said to be written by Thomas, Lord Wharton (1648-1715), set to the tune of a march with music attributed to English composer Henry Purcell (1659-1695). Although Purcell included it in a 1689 compilation as "a new Irish tune", he may well have appropriated the tune and claimed it as his own. The song also appears in Act 3 of *The Beggar's Opera* (1728) under the title *Lillibullero* with words by John Gay and sung by the character Macheath:

> *The Modes of the Court so common are grown*
> *That a true Friend can hardly be met:*
> *Friendship for Interest is but a Loan*
> *Which they let out for what they can get*

[See *How happy I could be with either.*] It is also featured as a recurrent theme in Laurence Sterne's novel *Tristram Shandy* (1759-67). The BBC World Service used the music for many years as its signature tune and stated on an internet site "that it started life as a jig with Irish roots", first appearing in 1661 in a collection published in London entitled "An Antidote Against Melancholy".

Lili Marlene (or *Lili Marleen*) is a German song, popular during World War II. Words written originally by German soldier-poet Hans Leip (1893-1983) in 1915, published in his collection of poetry in 1937 and set to music in 1938 by German composer Norbert Schultze (1911-2002). The song was originally called *Das Mädchen unter der Laterne* (*The Girl under the Lantern*) but became known as *Lili Marlene* or *Lili Marleen*. It was recorded in 1939 by

German chanteuse Lale Andersen (stage name of Eulalia or Liese-Lotte Bunneberg, 1905-1972). Despite efforts by the Nazi Minister for Propaganda Joseph Goebbels to suppress it, by 1941 it had become well-known among German troops because of its popularity with Field Marshall Rommel of the *Afrika Korps* when broadcast to North Africa over German-controlled Radio Belgrade. It was also sung by German-born Hollywood star Marlene Dietrich (1901-1992) who helped to popularize the song among Allied soldiers as a result of her numerous personal appearances before the troops and armed forces radio broadcasts, although her US commercial recording of the song (US Decca L3927) was not made until August 1945 (perhaps due to a strike of US musicians in 1942-44). The earliest English language recording was probably that of British singer Anne Shelton (1927-94) made in London on 9 May 1944 in a version translated by songwriters Tommie Connor and JJ Phillips and backed by Ambrose and his Orchestra (*qv.*) (UK Decca F8434). A little over a month later it was recorded by RCA in New York with vocals by Perry Como backed only by an unnamed chorus due to the US musicians' strike; that record (US Victor 20-1592) reached number 13 in the US Hit Parade.

Prince Igor
Opera by Russian composer Alexander Borodin (1833-87) first performed in 1890. It is based on the 12th century East Slavic epic, *The Tale of Igor's Campaign*. Borodin was also a member of a loose association of Russian musicians known as *"The Five"*. [See *Song of the Volga Boatmen*.] Moreland is reminded of the "cruel, parched, Central Asian feeling one gets from hearing" this opera when Matilda mentions the possibility of a production of Marlowe's *Tamburlaine the Great* (*CCR*, 55). Powell selected the *Polovtsian Dances* from this opera as one of his Desert Island Discs.

"Proms"
Popular name for the Promenade Concerts started in 1895 by Robert Newman (1858-1926) in the Queen's Hall, London (*qv.*) of which he was the manager, with Henry Wood (1869-1944) as conductor. They are so named because the audience were encouraged to walk around the concert hall during the performance. After the destruction of the Queen's Hall in a 1941 air raid, the concerts moved to the Albert Hall (*qv.*) where they continue to this day under the sponsorship of the BBC. The concerts were intended to enlist audiences from a broader spectrum of the population and this may explain why Mr Deacon attended and was encountered there "once or twice" by Gossage (*CCR*, 24).

PUCCINI, Giacomo (1858-1924)
Italian composer of several still popular operas, including *Tosca* (1900) and *Turandot* (1926) (*qv.*). General Conyers and Sir Gavin Walpole-Wilson once had "an argument over Puccini" at a dinner in one of the City livery

companies, "the Mercers – or was it the Fishmongers?" (*LM,* 84-85). [See also *"Baron Scarpia"*.]

Queen's Hall
Concert hall once located on Langham Place near Oxford Circus, London, opened in 1893. It was the original home of the Promenade Concerts (or "Proms") (*qv.*). It seated up to 3,000 and was considered to have nearly perfect acoustics. A single incendiary bomb destroyed it in 1941, and it was never rebuilt. It was the site of a Delius Festival discussed by Maclintick and Gossage at the Mortimer as part of their musical "shop" talk, causing Jenkins to "feel rather out of it" (*CCR,* 23). [See also DELIUS.] At dinner after the theatre, Matilda chides Moreland that Maclintick (one of the few critics who admires Moreland's music) would draw him to the Queen's Hall in a rickshaw if asked (*CCR,* 55). Moreland says that he first saw Dr Trelawney at a concert in this venue where the latter was pursuing his musical interests, which Moreland declares to be of the "most banal kind", by listening to *Death and Transfiguration* by Richard Strauss (*qv.*) (*KO,* 83).

Red Indian War Dance **
After moving to Castlemallock, the soldiers of Jenkins' unit suffer a lack of diversions formerly enjoyed. Consequently, a small group of them (lead by Williams, IG) engage in this "dance", witnessed by Jenkins and CSM Cadwallader:

> *The dancers, with tent-peg mallets for tomahawks, were moving slowly round in a small circle, bowing their heads to the earth and up again, as they gradually increased their speed of rotation.*

The dance seems to have been inspired more by exposure to Hollywood movies than to any anthropological studies of American aboriginal peoples. Jenkins wishes the unit's most noted dancer – Bithel – were present "to lead them in this dance" (*VB,* 174-75).

Reel
Type of folk dance and tune traditional in Scotland and Ireland, with slight differences between Scottish and Irish varieties. The form has also spread to England and other countries where Scots and Irish settled, such as the US and Canada. In the novel, Barbara Goring invites Nick Jenkins to visit her in Scotland where she says that a rival suitor, Johnny Pardoe (whom she eventually marries), plans to teach her to dance reels (*BM,* 64).

In Scotland the reel usually involves three or more pairs of dancers following a weaving path in and out of one another along a line completing a figure 8 pattern on the floor to music in 6 to 8 bars played in 4/4 or 2/4 time.

In his *Journals* Powell criticizes Edith Wharton's novel *The Buccaneers* (1938) for her British characters' expression of disdain for the high spirits and boisterousness of Americans practicing their own version of this dance, known as the Virginia Reel. Powell concluded that British characters would in fact be unlikely to adopt such a negative attitude to American dancers in view of their own horseplay in hunt ball reels such as Sir Roger de Coverley (*J90-92*, 31-32).

At the beginning of *QU* Nick Jenkins describes the dancers depicted in Poussin's painting, which provides the title for the series, as engaged in what sounds like some sort of reel:

> *the Seasons ... facing outward ... moving hand in hand in intricate measure; stepping slowly, methodically, sometimes a trifle awkwardly, in evolutions that take recognisable shape: or breaking into seemingly meaningless gyrations, while partners disappear only to reappear again, once more giving pattern to the spectacle: unable to control the melody, unable, perhaps to control the steps of the dance. (QU, 2)*

That is the same dance, perhaps the Reel of Life, in which the novels' characters will engage over the 12 volumes which follow. [See also Stag-Mask Dance.]

Requiem or German Requiem
Refers to *Ein Deutsches Requiem*, work for chorus, orchestra and soloists by Johannes Brahms (*qv.*), first performed in its entirety in 1868 (*SA*, 134).

The Ring of the Nibelung (or "The Ring")
Cycle of four operas written by Richard Wagner (*qv.*) consisting of *Rhinegold* (1869), *The Valkyrie* (1870), *Siegfried* (1876) and *The Twilight of the Gods* (1876). Brandreth refers to *The Ring* after encountering Jenkins, Moreland and Widmerpool in the nursing home where he is attending both Widmerpool and Isobel. After Widmerpool quickly rushes off from the encounter, Brandreth is reminded of the song (or *lied*) *Wanderlust* from the opera *Siegfried*, pedantically recalling both the English and German versions ("From the wood forth I wander, never to return", and *"Aus dem Wald fort in die Welt zieh'n: nimmer kehr' ich zurück"*). He regrets that none of the productions of *The Ring* he has attended fully reflect "the deeper pessimism of these words" (*CCR*, 104). After Brandreth departs, Moreland expresses thankfulness that Matilda is being attended by a non-music-loving gynaecologist (*CCR*, 105).

RUBINSTEIN, Ida (1885-1960)
Russian ballet dancer born into a wealthy Jewish family. At an early age she became an orphan, albeit an immensely rich one, and used her wealth to

promote her theatrical career. She debuted in 1909 in a "private" performance of Oscar Wilde's *Salomé* in St Petersburg (the production was effectively censored after the dress – or in this case, undress – rehearsal) in which she removed all seven of the veils in the dance of that name (*qv.*), wearing nothing at all by the time the performance was concluded. She also appeared in Paris with Serge Diaghilev's Russian Ballet (*qv.*) in 1909-10. In 1911, she appeared in her own Parisian production of *The Martyrdom of Saint Sebastian* (*qv.*) in which Gabriele d'Annunzio created for her the erotically-charged part of Saint Sebastian. Donners is said to have shed tears when watching Rubinstein's performance of this work. Sir Magnus most likely would have viewed Ida Rubinstein's later production of this play at Covent Garden in 1931. Matilda reportedly laughed at Donners' recounting of his emotional reaction (*HSH,* 50).

Russian Ballet (*Ballets Russes*)
Ballet company of Serge Diaghilev (*qv.*). When Jenkins visits Stringham's family during the Christmas school vacation, he is unable to accompany the family to a performance of the Russian Ballet because he has to join his parents in the country (*QU,* 56, 58, 60). However, the performance makes a sufficient impression on other members of the family for them to recall it in later years: Tuffy Weedon remembers, on re-encountering Jenkins at one of Lady Molly's parties in the 1930's, having been "put to all kinds of trouble to produce an extra ticket" for Stringham (*LM,* 161); and Mrs Foxe recalls the occasion a few years later at her party for Moreland's symphony, remarking that it was a pity Jenkins had not been able to accompany them (*CCR,* 141).

In his memoirs, Powell recalls attending a performance of *The Sleeping Princess* by the Russian Ballet in 1921, "while still a schoolboy" (*Faces,* 112). That was the year before the December 1922 events described in the novel. There is no record of a performance by the Russian Ballet in London in December 1922, so Powell seems to have transposed the historic event from his memory into the novel at a different time.

Jenkins cites the Russian Ballet as an important example of "intellectual emancipation" of its period (*LM,* 158). In his memoirs, Powell categorizes the Russian Ballet as "the most popularly recognized aspect of the burst of vitality in the arts that belongs to the first quarter of this century" (*Messengers,* 57).

The importance accorded by Powell to the Russian Ballet is consistent with the attitudes of Hugh Moreland and Constant Lambert to that group. Moreland's flat in Fitzrovia is decorated, *inter alia*, with "framed caricatures" of dancers from the early ballets of this company, including ballerinas Anna Pavlova (1881-1931) and Tamara Karsavina (1885-1978) and choreographer Michel Fokine (1880-1942), all Russian-born (*CCR,* 5). The heroine

(Barberina Rookwood) of Powell's last novel, *The Fisher King* (1986), is also a ballerina and is compared to, *inter alia*, Pavlova and Karsavina (*FK*, 211).

Diaghilev in 1925 commissioned Constant Lambert (see MORELAND: Source) at the age of 20 and while still a student to write the music for his ballet *Romeo and Juliet*. According to Powell's memoirs, the collaboration on this project was "volcanic", arising from problems over scenery design, with Diaghilev favouring surrealist painters Max Ernst (1891-1976) and Joan Miró (1893-1983) and Lambert favouring English artist Christopher Wood (1901-30) (originally selected by Diaghilev at Picasso's suggestion, only to be dismissed by Diaghilev without consulting Lambert). Another problem related to Lambert's dissatisfaction with unauthorized changes in the choreography of Bronislava Nijinska (1891-1972), sister of Vaslav Nijinski (*qv.*). The ballet was premiered in Monte Carlo in 1926 and then moved to Paris and London later in the year. Lambert and Diaghilev eventually patched up their quarrel but dealt with each other at arm's length thereafter and never again collaborated (*Messengers*, 57-58).

Le Sacre du Printemps (*The Rite of Spring*)
Music for the ballet by Russian composer Igor Stravinsky (1882-1971). It is one of the seminal modernist works of 20th century music and was first performed in Paris on 29 May 1913, by Serge Diaghilev's Russian Ballet (*qv.*) (*BDFR*, 119). [See also Existential Music.]

SAINT-SAËNS, Camille (1835-1921)
French composer who began his professional life as a pioneer, championing the music of the then radical works of Liszt and Wagner, but ending up seeming to be relatively conservative, opposed to the works of Debussy and Richard Strauss. His music is played on the 'cello by General Conyers who tells Jenkins that he isn't "getting on too badly with those arrangements of Saint-Saëns" (*LM*, 72). It is also played by

> *that favourite of Moreland's ... the pirate-like man with an old-fashioned wooden leg and patch over one eye, who used to scrape away at a fiddle in one of the backstreets off Piccadilly Circus.*

Jenkins is reminded of both of these musicians upon hearing the

> *strangled notes of the [Air Raid] Warning, as it died away, always recall[ing] some musical instrument inadequately mastered.*
> (*SA*, 6)

[See also "*Softly Awakes My Heart*" and STREET MUSICIANS.]

Santa Lucia
Traditional Neapolitan song extolling the virtues of the fishermen's district of that city in which a boatman extends an invitation to take a turn in his boat,

the better to enjoy the cool of the evening on the waters of the Bay of Naples. The song was transcribed and translated from Neapolitan dialect into Italian in 1849 during the early stages of the *Risorgimento*. The transcriber was Teodoro Cottrau (1827-1879) who is often credited as the composer. It is said to be the first Neapolitan song to be given Italian lyrics.

It is sung by the troupe of Venetian street singers as the concluding number of their performance near Jenkins' hotel that also included *Funiculì, Funiculà* (*qv.*). The entire troupe bursts into this song *en masse* while "the youngest and best-looking member" dubbed Soubrette by Dr Brightman, passes around a collection plate. Dr Brightman notes the incongruity of singing these Neapolitan songs in Venice, which she likens to "a Scotch ballad in Bath". She goes on to expatiate on Naples:

> *A taste for Naples is unique … You love the place, or you loathe it.*
> *The character of the traveller seems to have no bearing on the*
> *instinctive choice.* (*TK*, 18)

SARASATE, Pablo de (1844-1908)
Spanish violin virtuoso and composer. Full name Pablo Martin Meliton de Sarasate y Navascuéz. His performances were noted for the purity of their tone and avoidance of sentimentality. Much of his music was based on opera and was designed to enable him to demonstrate his mastery of technique in performance. According to Maclintick, Carolo performed works written or arranged by Sarasate while "playing ... up and down the country clad as Little Lord Fauntleroy" (*CCR*, 25).

SCHUBERT, Franz (1797-1828)
Austrian composer. He died at the relatively early age of 31. Brandreth compares his medical history to that of Wagner (*qv.*) and says that Schubert died of abdominal typhoid (*CCR*, 101). Other theories exist for his early death, including poisoning that might have resulted from the use of mercury in his treatment for syphilis from which he had suffered since 1822.

SCRIABIN, Alexander (1872-1915)
Russian composer and pianist. Among his compositions is *Le Poème de l'extase* (*The Poem of Ecstasy*), Opus 54, an orchestral piece, first performed in 1908. It was the subject of considerable controversy when performed by the Philadelphia Symphony Orchestra for the first time in 1919. Several members of the audience headed for the exits before the music even began, only to be scolded by conductor Leopold Stokowski for dismissing what he considered to be "one of the two best compositions written in modern times", and "one of the most highly organized and complex pieces of orchestral polyphony which exists". Constant Lambert describes the climaxes of this piece as "angry waves beating vainly at the breakwater of our intelligence"

(*Music Ho!* (London, 1985 edition), 261). Notwithstanding its somewhat out-of-the-ordinary character, Mrs Widmerpool, according to Moreland, who met her for the first time at a party at Lady Molly's, began on "Scriabin as soon as I arrived in the house" declaring that "*Poème de l'Extase* was her favourite musical work". Moreland comments that he himself has been "feeling ... far from *de l'extase*", which is not too surprising given that the war has just begun, Matilda has abandoned him, his landlord has turfed him out of his flat, and he has just been rescued by Lady Molly from a vet's office where he had taken his cat (Farinelli) to find it a new home (*KO*, 238, 242).

Second Piano Concerto
This is a reference to Piano Concerto No. 2 in B flat major (Op. 83) by Johannes Brahms (*qv.*). The concerto was first performed in Budapest in 1881 with Brahms himself playing the piano solo. Mr Deacon refers to Moreland's sentiments regarding the orchestration of this piece as one of Moreland's "youthful prejudices" (*CCR*, 13).

"*She'll be wearing purple socks, And she's always in the pox*"
Soldier's version of Irish folk song *Mick McGilligan's Daughter, Mary Anne*. Sung by the troops on the way to the Divisional hospital from the back of the truck also carrying Jenkins to Div HQ after they pass Maureen the barmaid who blows them a kiss (*VB*, 236). In the sanitized, non-military version by Louis A Tierney the socks rhyme occurs in the following lines:

> *And you'll know she's on the rocks*
> *When she's wearing cotton socks*

SHOSTAKOVITSCH, Dmitri (1906-75)
Russian composer active during the Soviet period. Maclintick considers him "Russia's only reputable post-Revolution composer" who was "not allowed to have his opera performed because the dictatorship of the proletariat finds that work musically decadent, bourgeois, formalist". Moreland, who declares himself somewhat "Pinkish" in his political views and longing to hear some "Marxist music", nevertheless declines to defend the Soviet regime and says that Shostakovitsch's suppressed second opera, *Lady Macbeth of the Mtsensk District*, is his "favourite title" (*CCR*, 120). The opera was first performed in Leningrad on January 22, 1934, and despite its popular success, was in 1936 denounced by the Communist party at Stalin's behest and afterwards suppressed. Shostakovitsch wrote a revised version, renamed *Katerina Ismailova*, first performed in 1962. The revisions were not intended to address the Stalinist criticisms to which the opera was earlier subjected. Although Shostakovitsch preferred the revised version, since his death the original version is more often performed.

SIBELIUS, Jean (1865-1957)

Finnish composer whose music such as *Finlandia* (1899-1900), played an important role in the formation of the Finnish national identity. He also wrote seven symphonies on which, together with his symphonic poems such as *Finlandia,* his reputation was largely based. He was a favourite of Audrey Maclintick's brother Stanley. It was Stanley's love of Sibelius' music that brought him together with Gossage who maintained his bank account at the branch where Stanley was a clerk. Their musical friendship, in turn, was the occasion for Maclintick's introduction to Audrey when the two of them joined Gossage and Stanley at a private performance of chamber music. Whether or not Sibelius was on the programme at this (for Maclintick) momentous concert is not stated in the novel (*CCR,* 208). However, the Maclintick character in the Channel 4 TV film says that he met Audrey at a Sibelius concert and then encountered her by chance a second time at a Richard Strauss (*qv.*) concert.

"Les Six"

An informal group of six composers working in Paris in the early 1920's:

> Georges Auric (1899-1983)
> Louis Durey (1888-1979)
> Arthur Honegger (1892-1955) (*qv.*)
> Darius Milhaud (1892-1974)
> Francis Poulenc (1899-1963)
> Germaine Tailleferre (1892-1983)

The group was put together by writer / filmmaker Jean Cocteau (1889-1963) in an attempt to promote himself as the leader of the musical avant-garde. The group adopted as its patron saint French composer and pianist Erik Satie (1866-1925). Their association, officially announced in 1920, was very short-lived and began to break up almost as soon as it was assembled. It produced an album of piano pieces (*Album des Six*) and collaborated on the incidental music for Cocteau's 1921 absurdist play *Les Mariés de la Tour Eiffel* (*Newlyweds on the Eiffel Tower*). Audrey is reported by Maclintick to be so adept at argumentation as to have made Gossage "contradict himself about his views on *Les Six*" (*CCR,* 210).

SLEZAK, Leo (1873-1946)

Opera singer (a tenor) and actor/comedian born in Šumperk, Moravia (then part of Austria-Hungary, now in the Czech Republic). He enjoyed particular success performing in the operas of Wagner and Verdi and was described by Powell in a 1938 review of his memoirs as a "great figure in international opera" ("Writers and Singers", *The Spectator*, 27 May 1938, 975-76). According to operatic lore, during a performance of Wagner's *Lohengrin* (*qv.*), a stagehand sent the swan out too early before Slezak could hop on board. As the swan disappeared backstage, he had to *ad lib* and came up with the line: *"Entschuldigen Sie, wann geht der nächste Schwan?"* (Sorry, what time's the next swan?). The line became so famous it was used by his son, film actor Walter Slezak (1902-83), as the title of his autobiography published in 1962. At the Walpole-Wilsons' dinner party, Sir Gavin interrupts an operatic conversation between Rosie Manasch and Johnny Pardoe with a statement that "No one could sing it like Slezak" (*BM*, 35). Pardoe then asks whether Sir Gavin had ever seen Slezak in *Lohengrin*, to which Sir Gavin "defiantly" responds "Many a time and oft" but then changes the subject to *Idomeneo* (*qv.*).

SMETANA, Bedřich (1824-1884)

Czech composer of, *inter alia*, the opera *The Bartered Bride* (*qv.*). At the London wartime performance of this work, Colonel Hlava informs Jenkins that Smetana's father made beer and wanted his son to do so as well "but Smetana instead made Czechoslovak national music" (*MP*, 97). His father was, indeed, a master brewer in Litomyšl, Bohemia, but was also an accomplished amateur violinist who gave Smetana lessons. Hlava also recalls that the British gave Smetana a musical degree (*MP*, 101), but he may have confused him in this regard with Dvořák (*qv.*) who was awarded an honorary degree by Cambridge University in 1891. Jenkins recollects an argument between Maclintick and Gossage about Smetana at Mrs Foxe's party on the occasion of Moreland's symphony (*MP*, 96-97). This may refer to what are characterized in the novel *CCR* as the "casual remarks" about this composer which Maclintick addressed to Gossage in that earlier context (*CCR*, 151).

"Softly Awakes My Heart" (*"Mon coeur s'ouvre á ta voix"*)

Aria (a mezzo-soprano part) from Act 2 of the opera *Samson et Dalila*, music by Camille Saint-Saëns (*qv.*), first performed in 1877; French libretto by Ferdinand Lemaire (*fl.* 1860's and 1870's), a Creole living in France who was related to Saint-Saëns by marriage. Moreland finds the street musician "with a peg leg and patch over one eye" [see STREET MUSICIANS] performing this song behind the London Pavilion (*qv.*) on his way to meet Jenkins at the Café Royal. He is cheered because this particular street musician, one of his favourites, is "still going" despite the disappearance of many others due to the war (*SA*, 114) .

"soldiers in the song ... fading away"

Jenkins is referring to the song *"Old Soldiers Never Die"* as he sees members of his unit beginning to leave the army after the surrender of Germany, in the "period between the Potsdam Conference and the dropping of the first atomic bomb" (*MP*, 198). The music for the song was written by Abby Hutchinson Patton (1829-1892) of the American singing group, the Hutchinson Family, active in the mid-19th Century. The song was published in New York in 1858 under the title *"Kind Words Can Never Die"*. British soldiers used that music for a song with their own words that was popular in WWI. One version of the soldiers' words went like this:

> *There is an old cookhouse, far far away*
> *Where we get pork and beans, three times a day.*
> *Beefsteak we never see, damn-all sugar for our tea*
> *And we are gradually fading away.*

> Chorus:
> *Old soldiers never die*
> *Never die, never die*
> *Old soldiers never die*
> *They just fade away.*

US General Douglas MacArthur (1880-1964) gave the song a revival when he quoted the last two lines of the chorus at the end of his speech to the US Congress after he was handed his papers in 1951 by President Harry S Truman for insubordination during the Korean War. Cowboy singing star Gene Autry recorded a new version of the song on that occasion intended to idolize MacArthur for his role in WWII, a point on which there is somewhat less than universal agreement. Another, less flattering song about the general circulated among the soldiers serving under his command in the Philippines after the Japanese invasion in 1941-42. It is sung to the tune of the *Battle Hymn of the Republic*:

> *Dugout Doug MacArthur lies ashakin' on the Rock*
> *Safe from all the bombers and from any sudden shock*
> *Dugout Doug is eating of the best food on Bataan*
> *And his troops go starving on.*

"So-let-each-cavalier-that-loves-honour-and-me" (Bonnie Dundee)
Poem by Sir Walter Scott (1771-1832) based on an incident arising from the calling of a Convention in Edinburgh by William of Orange to confirm his succession and involving Jacobite supporter John Graham of Claverhouse, 1st Viscount Dundee (circa 1648-89) aka. "Bonnie Dundee". It is sung to a traditional Scottish bagpipe air. Stringham hums this song in the manner in "which riders at a horse show might canter round the paddock" as he explains to Jenkins why he enlisted in the Army as an Other Rank (*SA*, 81). The lines recalled by Stringham come from the first verse:

> *To the Lords of Convention 'twas Claverhouse spoke;*
> *Ere the King's crown go down there are Crowns to be broke,*
> *Then each cavalier who loves honour and me,*
> *Let him follow the bonnets of Bonnie Dundee.*

"Some are sick, and some are sad"
Lines from the third verse of the hymn *At Even, Ere the Sun Was Set* (1868); words by English clergyman Henry Twells (1823-1900); it is set to various musical versions but Stringham probably sang it to the tune *Angelus* published by Georg Joseph of Breslau, Germany, in 1657, which seems to be the standard. At the Victory Thanksgiving Service Jenkins is reminded that Stringham was "addicted to quoting imagery [of hymns] within the context of his own life". He recalls that Stringham cited the words of this hymn as the best example of pronouncements "on the subject of one's friends and relations" (*MP*, 221-22). [See also *WN*, 110.] Stringham might well have gone on to recite the words from the next verse, "And some have friends who give them pain".

The Song of the Volga Boatmen
A well-known traditional Russian folk song collected by Russian composer Mily Balakirev (1837-1910), who also founded the loose association of Russian musicians known as "The Five". Other members of "The Five" included Cesar Cui (1835-1918), Modest Mussorgsky (1839-81) (according to Powell's memoirs, said by Constant Lambert to be the only person to have been given a less appropriate forename than himself (*Messengers,* 57), Nikolai Rimsky-Korsakov (1844-1908), as well as Alexander Borodin (who also wrote the opera *Prince Igor* (*qv.*)). The group was formed over the period 1856-62 to produce a distinctly Russian type of music, and their name inspired that later adopted by a group of Paris-based musicians known as "*Les Six*" (*qv.*).

The song was made popular by Feodor Chaliapin (*qv.*). A recording of the song by US band leader Glenn Miller (1904-44) became popular in the 1940's. Jenkins considers using this song as a test of Jimmy Brent's musical knowledge (*VB,* 130).

South of the Border
Title song for film featuring US cowboy star Gene Autry released in December 1939. Prior to the film's release, a UK recording was made in May 1939 by Henry Hall and the BBC Dance Orchestra, with vocals by Bob Mallin. Music by Michael Carr (1900-68) and words by Jimmy Kennedy (1902-84), both of whom were born and died in the UK

Upon reporting for duty in South Wales in December 1939, Jenkins hears the song sung by a barrack-room orderly (later identified as Jones, D.) as Jenkins is conducted around his new Company's billet by Lieutenant Idwal Kedward. Jenkins describes the music as "bursting gloriously from a hidden choir, a man's voice, deep throated and penetrating ... in a lament of heart-breaking melancholy". Another orderly joins in for the last two lines:

South of the border,
Down Mexico way. (*VB*, 4)

The singers (or Powell) confuse some of the words, for example, when
"*mañana*" is substituted for "*fiesta*". [See John Monagan, "Dance Music",
Anthony Powell Society Newsletter, 5 (Winter 2001), 5-6.[1]]

[See also Bernard Bergonzi, "Down Mexico way", *TLS*, 24/31 August 2007,
19. Note the later substitutions of "gown of white" for "veil of white" and
"stooped" for "knelt" which change the meaning of the song: "The Mexican
girl, having been abandoned by the gringo suitor, is becoming a nun".
Bergonzi attributes these substitutions to "Powell's misremembering".[2]]

Philip Larkin also noted that Powell had made a "slight mess" of the words of
this song to which Powell retorted, "they may well be, but I was not
reproducing the libretto, but roughly what the troops sang". [See Larkin,
Philip, *Required Writing* (London, 1983), 221; *J90-92, 71.*]

After being rebuked by Sergeant-Major Cadwallader for shirking their duties,
the soldiers continue to sing as they proceed to clean the barracks, "though
more restrainedly than before, perhaps because of the change of mood".
Jenkins is ruminating on how the lyrics of the song are matched by the actions
and moods of the soldiers just as Captain Gwatkin enters the room where
Jenkins meets him for the first time (*VB*, 6-7).

Stag-Mask Dance **

Pagan ritual dance performed by members of the Murtlock cult. The idea of
the performance seems to have originally occurred to Murtlock when he first
visited Jenkins' Somerset home and was told about The Devil's Fingers, a
Neolithic grave site consisting of "two worn [stone] pillars about five foot
high, and the same distance apart" located near Jenkins' home (*HSH*, 26).
The dance takes place on St John's Eve (or the Vigil of the Nativity of St John
the Baptist) which is June 23 in the Anglican Church calendar. There are four
and sometimes five dancers: Murtlock, Barnabas Henderson, Fiona Cutts,

---

[1] Monagan and his family also produced and presented to Powell a recording of this song
along with some others from the novels such as *Pale Hands* and *Guide Me, O Thou Great
Jehovah* which Powell thought offered a "rather refined rendering of the down-to-earth
singing of the Welsh troops, but interesting to hear collected together" (*J87-89, 131*).
[2] Bergonzi also refers to another contemporary recording of the song by Joe Loss and his
Orchestra with vocals by Monte Rey and remembers as a boy listening to the song on the
radio. He finds that the "introduction of the song brings in layers of cultural implications:
two British songwriters, one of them from Northern Ireland, tell a story of love and
betrayal in Mexico (which Jimmy Kennedy said had been inspired by a post card from
Tijuana), sung by a Welshman in wartime Britain as a „lament of heartbreaking
melancholy'. The incongruities underline a memorable moment in Powell's novel,
emphasizing the disruptions of time".

Rusty and, sometimes, Widmerpool, who also records the event on film. It is witnessed by Ernie Dunch, a local farmer, as well as Gwinnett. As described by Dunch (and recounted by Mr Gauntlett), it sounds somewhat like a primitive and seriously perverted version of the dance depicted in Poussin's painting that provides the title for the novels:

> *Dancing in and out o' the elder trees, and between Stones, it looked*
> *like, turning shoulder to shoulder t'ords each other, taking hold o'*
> *arms, shaking their heads from side to side.*

There are at least two male and two female dancers and sometimes a fifth, all naked. Dunch happens on the dance by accident and retreats quickly fearing he is in the presence of the devil (*HSH,* 157-59).

Gwinnett attends by invitation on the pretext that the dance is related to his research into early seventeenth century Gothicism. The ritual is, according to Gwinnett, intended "to summon up a dead man called Trelawney", but goes seriously wrong during the sexual invocations that follow on the dance (*HSH,* 164-69). Whether or what music may have guided the dance steps or on what instrument it may have been played does not seem to have occurred to either witness. The description of the dance in the novel may be to some extent inspired by an ancient dance surviving to the present day and known as the Horn or Antler Dance in which six dancers (all male) hold antlers (three painted red and three, white) to their heads as they dance. It is performed annually in Abbott's Bromley, Staffordshire, on the first Monday after 4 September. [See Reel.]

The Channel 4 TV film, perhaps not surprisingly, makes something of a meal out of this scene. There were four dancers, but no fifth dancer joins them, as in the novel, and neither Widmerpool nor Murtlock danced. There is a rudimentary rhythmical accompaniment on what sounds like a bongo drum played by another participant. Fortunately, the film viewer is spared the post-dance violence, where, in the novel, Murtlock gashes Widmerpool with a knife in a "part of the ritual [that] got out of hand ... some sort of struggle for power", according to Gwinnett, and the ceremony has to be abandoned (*HSH,* 168). In the TV film, after Widmerpool's death, Jenkins, who is Widmerpool's literary executor (a task he does not assume in the novels), finds the home movie version of the dance among Widmerpool's possessions and replays it in the final scene of the TV play.

STRAUSS, Richard (1864-1949)
German composer of late Romantic period best known for his operas and tone poems. Moreland attended a concert at Queen's Hall (*qv.*) in which Strauss' tone poem *Death and Transfiguration (Tod und Verklärung)* (1890) was performed. Dr Trelawney (who, according to Moreland, had "musical interests ... of the most banal kind") sat listening to this piece "with a

wonderfully fraudulent look on his face" (*KO,* 83). This is an orchestral work with an appropriately Trelawney-esque theme: it is a musical rendering of an artist's thoughts relating to his past life as he lay dying, at the end receiving the transfiguration for which he was longing. [See also *Funiculi, Funiculà* and *Dance of the Seven Veils.*]

STRAVINSKY, Igor (1882-1971)

Russian-born composer. Works include *Le Sacre du Printemps* (*qv.*). Norman Chandler, addressing Moreland in an encounter at the Mortimer, says that he has heard that Moreland "saw the new Stravinsky ballet when you were in Paris" (*CCR,* 21). Since this encounter takes place in about 1929, the "new" ballet referred to may be either *The Fairy's Kiss* (*Le Baiser de la Fée*), which was based on music by Tchaikovsky (*qv.*) and premiered in Paris on 27 November 1928, in a production by Ida Rubinstein's (*qv.*) company, or *Apollo* (*Apollon Musagète*), which had its Paris premiere on 12 June 1928 by the Russian Ballet (*qv.*) following its world premiere on 28 April 1928, at the Library of Congress, Washington, DC.

At about the same time, but in another novel and another time shift, Moreland ponders over how to succeed as a musical man of action, rejecting the alternative of composing "some ghastly, pretentious half-baked imitation of Stravinsky that makes a hit and is hailed as genius" (*KO,* 76).

STREET MUSICIANS

Crippled blonde singer ** Blonde woman on crutches, the "itinerant prima donna of the highways", who sings "*Pale hands I loved beside the Shalimar*" (*qv.*) on Gerrard Street, W1 (*CCR,* 1-3, 40). The singer and her song are remembered again by Moreland when Matilda has left him (*KO,* 249). During the war, Moreland mentions that he hasn't seen "the cantatrice on crutches for years" (*SA,* 114). However, she was still singing after the war, apparently after Moreland's death, when Jenkins hears her by the "vestigial remains of the Mortimer" (*CCR,* 2).

The crippled street singer was based on a real person:

> *Gerrard Street, in those days not wholly Chinatown, included Maxim's Chinese Restaurant, to some small extent model for Casanova's Chinese Restaurant, in the volume of that title. The street, something of a centre for itinerant musicians, at times echoed with the marvellous voice of the very pretty blonde crippled girl, with whose singing* <u>Casanova's Chinese Restaurant</u> *(1960) opens, though she is there represented as passing through another area of London, since she might suddenly appear in almost any neighbourhood. The blonde singer would certainly have been heard in opera had she not been lame.* (*Messengers,* 169)

She appears in the filmed version of *Dance* very briefly.

Old Venetian singer ** Performs *Funiculì Funiculà* (*qv.*) with a troupe at Jenkins' Venice hotel in 1958.

> *Hoarse, tottering, a few residual teeth … he rendered the song in*
> *slower time than ordinary, clawing the air with his hands, stamping*
> *the floor with his feet, while he mimed the action of the cable.*
> (*TK,* 1, 240)

[See also *Santa Lucia.*]

One-eyed peg-leg fiddle player ** Street musician, "a favourite of Moreland's", who "used to scrape away at a fiddle in one of the backstreets off Piccadilly Circus" (*SA,* 6). During the war Moreland observes him behind the London Pavilion, "playing *Softly Awakes My Heart* (*qv.*). Rather an individual version" (*SA,* 114). [See also *WN, 85* where an unidentified man is said to be seen playing the same tune on an accordion.]

The Soubrette ** "The youngest and the best looking of the troupe" that sings *Funiculì Funiculà* (*qv.*) in Venice in 1958 (*TK,* 18). Named by Dr Emily Brightman, who wonders if she is mistress or great-granddaughter to the old Venetian singer (*qv.*) (*TK,* 4). [See also *Santa Lucia.*]

Predecessors Powell also referred to street musicians in his pre-*Dance* novels, most notably in *From a View to a Death* (1933) where there are some street musicians called the Orphans, which as a group, become rather prominent secondary characters. The group consists of three brothers, now middle-aged but orphaned in their youth, who wander about the town near Passenger Hall playing songs on their "organ" (presumably a hurdy-gurdy). One plays while the others importune passers-by for donations. They perform a fairly extensive repertoire in the novel, including two songs which come close to being mentioned in *Dance* – *Barcarolle* (see *Tales of Hoffmann*) and *O sole mio* (which was surely among the songs offered by the Venetian Street Musicians). The Orphans are hired by Torquil Fosdick to provide entertainment at his cocktail party at the Fox and Hounds, but with disastrous results – one of them drinks too much and makes a pass at one of the female guests. Their music is also heard in the background by various characters throughout the novel (*FVD,* 16, 18-20, 57, 81, 110-24, 210).

In *Afternoon Men* (1931) a street musician playing *Ah, Sweet Mystery of Life* on a cornet is heard outside a pub called the Plumbers' Arms (*AM,* 120). There is also a troupe of street actors at the beginning of *Agents and Patients* (1936) which performs without music before a group of spectators that includes several of the characters; their act involves a partnership with one in chains and the other collecting money from the crowd to help his partner gain release. Maltravers manages an allusion to the *Eton Boating Song,* commenting "it certainly looks as if nothing would sever the [chain] that is round him now". It occurs to Chipchase that a better performance was offered by "the organ and the transvest dancers", apparently in another group (*A&P*, 4-10). Powell recalls this incident as having taken place "at the east end of Gerrard Street, in the open space behind the Shaftesbury Theatre" (*Messengers*, 10). [See also *WN*, 20 (A beggar playing Rubinstein's *Melody in F* on a violin).]

Tales of Hoffmann

Opera (*Les contes d'Hoffmann* in French) by German-born composer Jacques Offenbach (1819-1880), who spent most of his professional life in France. It was first performed in Paris in 1881 a few months after the composer's death. The libretto was based on three stories by German writer of the Romantic era ETA Hoffmann (1776-1822). Priscilla Tolland suggests that the music from this opera (which she calls *Tales from Hoffmann*) would have been preferable to the military marches from which a friend of Audrey Maclintick's suffered when played on the gramophone by her former husband at 4 AM (*CCR*, 174). In a later novel, orchestral music from this opera is being played in Venice by a caffè orchestra as the "Stevens party withdrew" from their encounter with Jenkins, Gwinnett and Pamela at Florian's in the Piazza San Marco (*TK*, 169). In both cases, the music referred to may well have been the *Barcarolle* from Act 3 which is the most well-known piece from this work and was based on a folk song of Venetian gondoliers.

Tango

A dance, originating in the *demi-monde* of Buenos Aires brothels. The music is a fusion of European, African and South American Milonga rhythms. The term "tango" began to be applied in the 1890's, and it spread to Europe in the early years of the 20th Century. It exists in various styles but the one referred to in the novel would most likely be the "International" (English) style, which was a simplified, ballroom variation. It was "codified" in 1922 when it was limited to modern music, ideally at 30 bars to the minute (*ie*. 120 beats per minute – assuming a 4/4 measure). It is danced by a couple, frequently incorporating a staccato movement and characteristic "head snaps", which are foreign to the Argentine original. Jenkins' mother comments about Bertha Conyers that her stories, while amusing, are not reliable, "especially the one about Mrs Asquith and the man who asked her if she danced the tango" (*KO*, 40). [See also *Tess of Le Touquet*.]

Tannhäuser

German mediaeval legend and opera based on that legend by Richard Wagner (*qv*.) entitled *Tannhäuser und der Sängerkrieg auf der Wartburg* (*Tannhäuser and the Singers' Contest on the Wartburg*), first performed in 1845. In the legend, a poet knight, Tannhäuser, discovers the subterranean lair of Venus (the "Venusberg") where he spends a year worshipping the Goddess. He leaves filled with remorse and seeks forgiveness from the Pope for having worshipped a pagan Goddess; but the Pope tells him that such forgiveness is as impossible as it would be for his staff to take root and bloom. After the knight leaves Rome for the Venusberg, the staff sprouts leaves, a sign that he has received God's forgiveness. In his opera, Wagner adds to this legend another story about a singers' contest on the Wartburg, near the legendary location of the Venusberg in Thuringia.

In the novel, reference is made to the story of the Venusberg. Jenkins is reminded of that story when Widmerpool describes a postcard from Pamela in Cairo, which he received, "in that basement where I work night and day", meaning the Cabinet War Office constructed below the buildings of Whitehall. Jenkins recalls a description of the Venusberg in a poem by John Davidson [See SPURLING, Book Index] where the lovers

> *wait, while empires sprung*
> *Of hatred thunder past above*
> *Deep in the earth for ever young*
> *Tannhäuser and the Queen of Love.*

Jenkins recognizes that the analogy is somewhat strained, since Pamela is unlikely to have visited Widmerpool in his underground offices.

> *On the other hand, she herself could easily be envisaged as one of*
> *the myriad incarnations of Venus, even if Widmerpool was no*
> *Tannhäuser.* (*MP*, 203)

In his *Journals* Powell used the same quote from Davidson's poem to describe his friends the Spurlings, after a 1985 visit to their new house in Holloway, North London (at that time a "pioneering district for intellectuals"), as living "in a sense ‚deep in the earth, forever young', like Tannhäuser and the Queen of Love" (*J82-86,* 144).

The title and epigraph of Powell's second novel *Venusberg* (1932) also refer to this legendary mountain. The hero of that novel leaves London for a sojourn in an unnamed Baltic city (incorporating elements of both Helsinki and Talinn) where he encounters a new love interest in a romantic setting somewhat reminiscent of Tannhäuser's Venusberg. The city is adorned with

> *blue-green spires and a red and gold cathedral. A castle or palace*
> *in grey stone was built on a rampart in a part of the town that was*
> *on a higher level than the rest of the houses. (V, 39)*

TCHAIKOVSKY, Peter Ilyich (1840-93)

Russian composer of orchestral music, operas and ballets, including such still popular examples of the latter as *Sleeping Beauty, Swan Lake* and *The Nutcracker*. Moreland's uncle drank a glass of wine with the composer at

Cambridge where he received an honorary degree (*CCR*, 4). This was a Doctor of Music awarded in 1893, just a few months before he died in November of that year. At the same time, degrees were conferred upon Saint-Saens (*qv*.) and Grieg (*qv*.).

The music from Tchaikovsky's ballet, *Swan Lake,* is the work being played (badly) by the ship's orchestra in *The Fisher King* (1986) when Barberina Rookwood returns to the saloon and begins to dance, signifying her break with Saul Henchman (*FK,* 208-09).

Te Deum
Canticle sung before *God Save the King* (*qv*.) at the Victory Thanksgiving Service (*MP*, 226). Also known as *Te deum laudamus* (and so described in the service sheet), the *Ambrosian Hymn*, or *A Song of the Church*. The original words are sometimes ascribed to Saints Ambrose and Augustine on the occasion of the latter's baptism of the former in 387 AD. It may be sung to plainsong, Anglican chant or to various choral settings. The setting used at the Victory Service is not specified, but it would most probably have been one of the choral settings in the choir's usual repertoire, or simply sung to Anglican chant.

Tess of le Touquet **
A song performed by Max Pilgrim at Mrs Andriadis' party. The lyrics are reproduced in the novel as he sang them (*BM,* 115, 118, 120). The homosexual references in the lyrics inflame Mr Deacon, and this results in a serious contretemps between him and Max as the party is drawing to a close, ultimately resulting in Mr Deacon being banned from the party by the hostess (*BM,* 148-151). The song is reminiscent of Walton's (*qv*.) *Tango-Pasodoblé* in his musical version of Edith Sitwell's *Façade:*

> *the lady and her friend from Le Touquet*
> *In the very shady trees upon the sand*
> *Were plucking a white satin bouquet*
> *While the sand's brassy band*
> *Blared in the wind.*

In the Channel 4 TV film, there being no music for the fictional *Tess of le Touquet,* the producers substituted *There Are Fairies at the Bottom of our Garden,* sung by TV actor Grant Parsons in a camp manner sufficiently pronounced to enrage Mr Deacon. That song was written by Liza Lehmann (1862-1918), English born singer and composer to words by Rose Fyleman (1877-1957).

"There's a Long, Long Trail A Winding"
Song popular among American and British soldiers during World War I. Published in 1913, with words by Stoddard King (1889-1933) and music by

Alonzo "Zo" Elliott (1891-1964), both Americans and both educated at Yale University. The chorus is sung by Ted Jeavons in a "full, deep unexpectedly attractive voice, so different from the croaking tones in which he ordinarily conversed" after his brother, Stanley, tells Jenkins that he can get him into the regiment of his choice (but which is not named in the novel) (*KO,* 254). [See also *WN,* 105.]

In his memoirs, Powell recounts a dinner at his neighbours in Somerset to which Maurice Bowra (1898-1971) was invited as a house guest of the Powells. After the meal

> *Bowra insisted – he really did insist – on the whole party spending the rest of the evening singing „There's a long, long trail a-winding' and „Pack up your troubles in your old kit bag'.*

This was offered as evidence of how much the first war had meant to Bowra (*Infants,* 192-93). Bowra served in the war after matriculating at New College, Oxford and returned to complete his studies after his war service ended. In 1922 he became a fellow of Wadham College, and held the position of Dean of that college when Powell met him during Powell's undergraduate days at Balliol College in 1923-26 (*Infants,* 178). Bowra was near enough in age to mix freely with the undergraduates of Powell's era (he was only about eight years older than Powell) but, unlike them, was deeply affected by his participation in WWI (*Infants,* 182-83). He became Warden of Wadham College in 1938 and held that post for the rest of his life. He was knighted in 1951.

Tone Poem Vieux Port **
[See MORELAND: Works.]

Torch Dance
A dance originating in Scotland but popularised in Germany in around 1821 when it was revived at Berlin as the "royal dance of torches". It is apparently this dance to which Sir Gavin Walpole-Wilson refers as having been performed by "The King and the Tsar ... with the bride between them. A splendid sight" (*BM,* 48).

TOSCANINI, Arturo (1867-1957)
Italian conductor, reputed to be the greatest of his era. In the context of a discussion involving Jenkins, Moreland and both of the Maclinticks, Audrey baits her husband by charging that he approved of (or at least failed to find objectionable) an attack on Toscanini, when "The Fascists slapped his face", probably referring to an incident in Bologna in 1931 when he was assaulted by Fascist thugs. After that, Toscanini refused to play again in Italy. He withdrew from Germany in 1933 and abandoned Austria as well, after 1938. Maclintick denies Audrey's charge of Fascist sympathies, reminding her that

he himself was taken to a police station in Florence by a Blackshirt when Audrey "tried to truckle to him" (*CCR,* 120-21).

"Trumpeter, what are you sounding now?"

First line from 1904 song *The Trumpeter*, words by Francis Barron (1868-1940), music by J Airlie Dix (d. 1911). Umfraville recalls the song after a bad day at the races (*TK,* 3). He thinks the Trumpeter is calling "*Defaulter*s" [See Bugle Calls] but in the song the calls mentioned are *Reveille, Charge* and *Rally.* The last verse goes as follows:

> *Trumpeter, what are you sounding now?*
> *(Is it the call I'm seeking?)*
> *"Lucky for you if you hear it at all*
> *For my trumpet is faint in speaking,*
> *I'm calling ,em home! Come home! Come home!*
> *Tread light o'er the dead in the valley,*
> *Who are lyin' around face down to the ground,*
> *And they can't hear me sound the ,Rally'.*
> *But they'll hear it again in a grand refrain,*
> *When Gabriel sounds the last ,Rally'."*

Turandot

Opera written by Italian composer Giacomo Puccini (*qv.*) and first performed in 1926 at La Scala in Milan. Matilda Moreland says that it was after attending a performance of this opera that Buster Foxe pinched her leg, causing her to turn against the Foxe household (*CCR,* 135, 147). It is one of Sir Magnus Donners' favourites. Matilda recalls, with derision, the tears Donners shed at the suffering of the Chinese slave girl. This refers to Liu, a young Chinese slave girl, who commits suicide in Act III, Scene 1, rather than reveal the name of her beloved (The Unknown Prince) to the cruel Chinese Princess, Turandot. Puccini did not live to complete the opera, but the portions he did complete include the arias sung by the Chinese slave girl which so moved Sir Magnus (*HSH,* 50).

"the vintage, where the Grapes of Wrath were stored"

Moreland recites this phrase from *The Battle Hymn of the Republic* by American abolitionist and political activist Julia Ward Howe (1819-1910) in response to Jenkins' reference to a parade of vintage cars then taking place outside Moreland's South London hospital. Moreland recalls that one stood upright in "the tradesman's van of Edwardian date or earlier", in which he presumes the vintage of the Grapes of Wrath would have been stored (or, possibly, transported) (*TK,* 276). The music was written in the 1850's by William Steffe as a religious camp meeting song and was used for various popular songs, including the still familiar *John Brown's Body.* When Mrs Howe heard that version being sung during the War Between the States, she was inspired to write new words that became popular during that war as *The Battle Hymn of the Republic*. It has remained on the US repertory of patriotic songs ever since. [See also Revelation 14:18-19.]

WAGNER, Richard (1813-1883)

German composer and conductor. Moreland's uncle heard Wagner conduct at the Albert Hall (*qv.*) which was opened in 1871 (*CCR,* 4). Wagner conducted a series of concerts at the Royal Albert Hall in 1877 to raise money to cover deficits at Bayreuth, and it may have been one of these that Moreland's uncle attended. His most noted work is the operatic cycle *The Ring of the Nibelung* (*qv.*). A character in that work is Mime (*qv.*) whose name is applied by Jenkins to an officer in MIL sharing certain physical characteristics. Jenkins is reminded of the music and story of *The Ring* when he encounters this officer on several occasions. Wagner also wrote the opera *Parsifal* (*qv.*), one of Sir Magnus Donner's favourites, as well as *Tannhäuser* (*qv.*).

Brandreth [see MUSIC LOVERS] recounted Wagner's medical history when he encountered Jenkins, Moreland, and Widmerpool in the nursing home where Jenkins was visiting Isobel. He tells them that Wagner suffered his entire life from erysipelas, a disease of the skin causing inflammation and fever, but finally died of a heart attack. He then extends this exhibition of his knowledge of composers' maladies by contrasting Wagner's death to that of Schubert (*CCR,* 101). [See also "*The Ring of the Nibelung*".] Moreland sends Jenkins a post card with a picture of Wagner "in a kind of tam-o-shanter" to confirm their dinner at the Café Royal (*SA,* 92).

Wagnerian castle

Refers to *Schloss Neuschwanstein* ("New Swan-Stone Castle") built in Bavaria by King Ludwig II (1845-86, reigned 1864-1886) and opened shortly after his death. It was named for Lohengrin, the Swan Knight (*der Schwanenritter*, in German) hero of Wagner's 1850 opera of the same name (*qv.*). The castle incorporates several Wagnerian elements, including wall paintings depicting scenes from his operas as well as several rooms designed as settings for various scenes from his operas, particularly *Tannhäuser* (*qv.*) and *Lohengrin* (*qv.*). Ludwig II was an admirer of Wagner and provided financial support for the construction of the Bayreuth *Festspielhaus* (Festival Hall) as well as the completion of some of Wagner's later operas such as *Parsifal* (*qv.*) and some of the *Ring Cycle* (*qv.*). The castle is festooned with fanciful turrets and other Victorian-era bric-a-brac in a "fairyland" style that has strongly influenced the design for the "Sleeping Beauty" castles in various Walt Disney venues around the world. Moreland somewhat exaggeratedly refers to Magnus Donners' castle at Stourwater as of the same category as *Neuschwanstein:* a palace in which Ludwig II "wouldn't have been ashamed to disport himself" (*KO,* 96). When the Morelands and the Jenkinses arrive at Stourwater, Moreland exclaims: "I told you it was

Wagnerian" (*KO*, 106). While Moreland may be correct in characterizing Stourwater as exhibiting some Wagnerian features, they are unlikely to have risen to the level manifested by *Neuschwanstein.*

WALTON, Sir William, OM (1902-83)

English composer. He was for a time a lodger of the literary Sitwell family in Osbert Sitwell's London residence at 2 Carlyle Square, Chelsea; according to Powell, who met him there, Walton was "more or less one of the family". He was an Oxford contemporary of Sacheverell Sitwell, who, Powell says, first recognized Walton's "musical inspiration" (*Messengers,* 39-41). Powell was interviewed in 1985 for a television programme about Walton, with particular reference to his relationship with Constant Lambert, but the interview was not included in the final version of the programme (*J82-86,* 148). Walton's setting to music of poems from Edith Sitwell's collection *Façade* (1922-23) brought him notice as a musical modernist. [See *Tess of le Touquet.*] At the end of the Victory Thanksgiving Service, the Welsh Guards played what Jenkins describes as "Walton's „Grand March'", which he deems to be "something in Moreland's line" (*MP*, 227). He is referring to Walton's march *Crown Imperial*, commissioned by the BBC for and played at the coronation of George VI in 1937.

Waltz

Dance step to music in 3/4 time which became popular in Vienna in the 1780's and remains a standard in ballroom dancing today. It is performed in a closed position of two dancers, with the most common configuration involving a full turn in two bars using three steps per bar. Widmerpool's favourite music is a waltz, in which he engaged Barbara Goring to become his dance partner at the Huntercombes' ball, with disastrous results (*BM*, 65, 70-71; *TK*, 158).

In his memoirs, Powell recalls an incident on a Mediterranean cruise when his wife danced a waltz (*The Blue Danube*) with Maurice Bowra (who lectured on such cruises when he was not performing his duties at Oxford) which was "the sole dance he recognized ... pawing the ground like a little bull entering the ring" (*Infants*, 193). [See also *"There's A Long, Long Trail A-Winding"*.]

Water Music

A collection of orchestral movements composed by GF Handel (*qv.*) for King George I (1660-1727, reigned 1714-27) and premiered in 1717 on a barge floating on the Thames (*MP*, 218). This piece was also one of those chosen by Constant Lambert to be played at the Powells' wedding service at All Saints, Ennismore Gardens, near Rutland Gate where Lady Violet was living at the time and located near the Royal Albert Hall (*Faces*, 17-18). The church is still functioning as the Russian Orthodox Cathedral of The Dormition of the

Mother of God and All Saints, Ennismore Gardens, London, SW7. [See also *Wedding March*.]

Wedding March
Played at the conclusion of the Akworth-Cutts wedding ceremony near Stourwater (*HSH,* 194). Probably the "Wedding March", sometimes referred to as the "Bridal March", by German composer Felix Mendelssohn (1809-47) who wrote it in 1842 as incidental music to accompany performances of Shakespeare's *A Midsummer Night's Dream.* It was popularized for English weddings by its selection for the wedding of Queen Victoria's daughter to the Crown Prince of Prussia in 1858.

"Wedding March" is sometimes also the name applied to the "Bridal Chorus" from the opera *Lohengrin* by Richard Wagner (*qv.*) – the familiar "Here comes the bride" – but that tune is usually played as the processional at the beginning of English weddings, whereas the tune heard by Jenkins is played at the end of the ceremony, when the Mendelssohn piece would be the more preferred choice for the recessional. At the Powells' wedding on 1 December 1934, Constant Lambert chose the music and insisted on the Wagnerian *Wedding March* rather than Mendelssohn's version, "but was himself too incapacitated by the party [on the previous evening at Powell's Brunswick Square flat] to attend the church" (*Faces,* 18). The Wagnerian version is also played at the wedding which takes place in the Guards' Chapel at the beginning of Powell's pre-war novel *What's Become of Waring* (*WBW,* 2).

"We had ter join Belisha's army"
World War II soldier's song referring to Leslie Hore-Belisha, 1st Baron Hore-Belisha (1893-1957), Liberal and Liberal National MP who became Secretary of State for War in 1937 under the government of Neville Chamberlain. He was responsible for introducing conscription, first proposing it unsuccessfully in 1938 but finally succeeding in early 1939 as the threat from Nazi Germany worsened. The song is sung by the troops following *Guide Me, O Thou Great Jehovah* (*qv.*) as they march to their transport for movement from South Wales to Northern Ireland in December 1939, just prior to Hore-Belisha's dismissal from the War Office in January 1940 (*VB,* 40). There is independent corroboration that such a song was circulating among British troops in 1939-40, with words considerably more bawdy than those recorded in *VB.* [See for example, Martin Page, *Kiss Me Goodnight, Sergeant-major: the songs and ballads of World War II* (London, 1973).] What tune was used for the song is not mentioned either in the novel or the collection of soldiers' songs.

Another soldier's song referring to Hore-Belisha was banned by his order while still at the War Office in the early months of the war, the anti-Semitic tenor of the lyrics probably contributing to the suppression order:

Onward Christian soldiers
You have nought to fear.
Israel Hore-Belisha
Will lead you from the rear.
Clothed by Monty Burton,
Fed on Lyons pies;
Die for Jewish freedom
As a Briton always dies.

Wein, Weib und Gesang

Waltz (Op. 333) by Austrian composer Johann Strauss the Younger (1825-99), also known as the Waltz King. The name in English is *Wine, Women and Song*. It was originally written as a choral waltz, commissioned by a Viennese choral society where it was first performed in 1869. The title is taken from a German proverb based on a Biblical passage that is also referring to the elements of an enjoyable life (at least from a masculine perspective): *Wer nicht liebt **Wein, Weib** und **Gesang**, der bleibt ein Thor sein Leben lang* (German proverb alluding to Martin Luther's Bible) "Those who don't enjoy wine, women and song remain fools for life". [See BIBLE: *Ecclesiastes* 8:15: "a man hath no better thing under the sun than to eat, and to drink and to be merry".] Moreland refers to this waltz, or the philosophy of life it represents, when he is accompanying Jenkins on the way to see Maclintick. After stating that Maclintick probably hates women, "only likes whores", Moreland concludes: "All the same, Maclintick is also full of romantic, hidden away sentiments about *Wein, Weib und Gesang*" (*CCR*, 107).

"We'll have a – Blue Room – | New Room for – two room –"

Lines from Broadway show tune *The Blue Room* by Rodgers and Hart published in 1926. [See *My Heart Stood Still*.] It was used in the Broadway musical *The Girl Friend* (1926) and in their London bedroom farce *Kitty's Kisses* (1927). Subsequently, it was also used in the movie *Words and Music* (1948), which was based on the lives of Rodgers and Hart. At the Huntercombes' dance, those choosing to go out into the garden of Belgrave Square for a breath of fresh air could hear "rival bands" playing this song from one ballroom and *Mountain Greenery* (*qv.*) (also a Rodgers and Hart song) from another (*BM*, 62-63).

"When Father went down to Southend"

Lines from the music hall song entitled *Father Went Down to Southend*, written by TW Connor (d. 1936) and published in 1911. It was sung by Dan Crawley. Connor was also the author of such other popular music hall standards as *A Little Bit of Cucumber* (1915) and *She Was One of the Early Birds* (1895). Ted Jeavons sings the chorus of the song in a "mellow, unexpectedly attractive voice" as he makes a list of those who sent wreaths to Erridge's funeral (*BDFR*, 90-91).

"When I tread the verge of Jordan"
[See *Guide Me O Thou Great Jehovah*.]

"Whom do you lead on Rapture's roadway, far, | Before you agonize them in farewell?"
[See "*Pale hands I loved beside the Shalimar*".]

Wigmore Hall
Concert hall on Wigmore Street near the Wallace Collection in Marylebone, London. Originally called Bechstein Hall, it was built in 1901 by the Bechstein piano company of Germany. It was closed at the outset of WWI in response to anti-German sentiment but reopened in 1917 and renamed Wigmore Hall (in response to the same sentiment that motivated the Royal Family to change their name from the House of Saxe-Coburg-Gotha to the House of Windsor). It has a capacity of about 560 seats and is used primarily for the performance of chamber music and recitals. Moreland first heard Carolo (*qv.*) perform in this hall, almost the first public musical performance he can remember (*CCR*, 20).

WISE, Rupert **
Dancer, "known for his strict morals and lack of small talk"; a friend of Norman Chandler who describes him as having "a profile like Apollo but ... a mind like Hampstead Garden Suburb"; appears at Mrs Foxe's party for Moreland (*CCR*, 142-43).

"You make fast, I make fast, make fast the dinghy"
Song of the Royal Engineers (or Sappers) based on the traditional South African song *Daer de die ding* or *Marching to Pretoria*. In the official version "clay" is sung instead of "shit" in the final line of the refrain quoted in the novel. Lafflan's Plain refers to a training area at Aldershot, which is where this song is sung, appropriately enough, by a detachment of Sappers who march past Jenkins as he reminisces with Jimmy Brent. The song brings to a close the scene in which Jenkins learns more details of the cause of his break-up with Jean Duport and seems "not only the battle hymn of warring tribes, but also ... a general lament for the emotional conflict of men and women" (*VB*, 134).

Appendix A: Anthony Powell's Desert Island Discs

Broadcast: 16 October 1976 on BBC Radio Four

Powell chose the following:

Discs:

1. *If You were the Only Girl in the World,* performed by Violet Loraine & George Robey.

2. *Were I Laid on Greenland's Coast* from John Gay's *The Beggar's Opera,* performed by Elsie Morison and John Cameron, with the *Pro Arte* Orchestra, Malcolm Sargent conducting.

3. Verdi's *La donna e mobile* from *Rigoletto,* performed by Luciano Pavarotti, with the London Symphony Orchestra, Richard Bonynge conducting.

4. Strauss's *Tales from the Vienna Woods,* performed by the Vienna Philharmonic, Willi Boskovsky conducting.

5. Borodin's *Polovtsian Dances* from *Prince Igor,* performed by the Berlin Philharmonic, Herbert von Karajan conducting.

6. Constant Lambert's *The Rio Grande,* performed by the Hallé Orchestra (with soloists and chorus), Constant Lambert conducting.

7. Milhaud's *La création du monde,* performed by *Orchestre du Théâtre des Champs-Élysées,* Darius Milhaud conducting.

8. Debussy's *Iberia* from *Images for Orchestra No. 2,* performed by *Orchestre de la Suisse Romande,* Ernest Ansermet conducting.

Book: Lermontov's *A Hero of Our Time.*

Luxury: One bottle of red wine every day.

Source:
Desert Island Lists by Roy Plomley with Derek Drescher, Hutchinson, 1984.
Anthony Powell Society Newsletter, **22** (supplied by Robert Greenwood of Chatham, Kent).

Appendix B: Service Sheet for Victory Thanksgiving Service, St Paul's Cathedral, London, 19 August 1945

St. Paul's Cathedral

A
SERVICE OF THANKSGIVING
TO
ALMIGHTY GOD

for the Victory granted to Britain and her Allies

SUNDAY, 19th, AUGUST, 1945

While the Congregation are assembling the following music shall be played by the

Band of the WELSH GUARDS :

First Suite in ' E ' Flat ... ... *Holst*
" Nimrod " from the Enigma Variations ... *Elgar*
Lyric Suite ... ... *Grieg*
The Royal Water Music ... ... *Handel*

During the retirement of Their Majesties the Band shall play :
Grand March—" Crown Imperial " ... *Walton*

Order of Service

At the entrance of Their Majesties to the Cathedral a Fanfare sounds from the steps of the Cathedral.

During the Procession from the West Door, and while Their Majesties and the Archbishop and Clergy are taking their places, the Band plays.

Then follows the BIDDING spoken by the Dean, the Congregation standing.

BRETHREN, we are met together on this day to pour out our hearts in fervent thanksgiving to the God and Father of us all, and to dedicate ourselves afresh to the service of his Kingdom. We desire to thank him for deliverance from the hand of our enemies ; for the devotion, even to death, of those who through the years of war have stood between us and slavery ; and for the hopes of a better world for all his people. I bid you, therefore, lift up your hearts that you may tell the praises of our God, and pray that his wisdom may lead us, and his spirit strengthen us, in the days that are to come.

HYMN

PRAISE my soul, the King of Heaven,
   To his feet thy tribute bring ;
Ransom'd, heal'd, restored, forgiven,
   Evermore his praises sing ;
      Alleluia ! Alleluia !
   Praise the everlasting King.

Praise him for his grace and favour
   To our fathers in distress ;
Praise him still the same as ever,
   Slow to chide, and swift to bless ;
      Alleluia ! Alleluia !
   Glorious in his faithfulness.

Father-like, he tends and spares us,
   Well our feeble frame he knows ;
In his hands he gently bears us,
   Rescues us from all our foes ;
      Alleluia ! Alleluia !
   Widely yet his mercy flows.

Angels in the height, adore him ;
   Ye behold him face to face ;
Saints triumphant, bow before him,
   Gather'd in from every race,
      Alleluia ! Alleluia !
   Praise with us the God of Grace.

3

THE LESSON : ISAIAH, Chapter 35.

THE wilderness and the solitary place shall be glad for them ; and the desert shall rejoice, and blossom as the rose.

It shall blossom abundantly, and rejoice even with joy and singing : the glory of Lebanon shall be given unto it, the excellency of Carmel and Sharon, they shall see the glory of the Lord, and the excellency of our God.

Strengthen ye the weak hands, and confirm the feeble knees.

Say to them that are of a fearful heart, Be strong, fear not : behold, your God will come with vengeance, even God with a recompence : he will come and save you.

Then the eyes of the blind shall be opened, and the ears of the deaf shall be unstopped.

Then shall the lame man leap as an hart, and the tongue of the dumb sing : for in the wilderness shall waters break out, and streams in the desert.

And the parched ground shall become a pool, and the thirsty land springs of water : in the habitation of dragons, where each lay, shall be grass with reeds and rushes.

And an highway shall be there, and a way, and it shall be called The way of holiness ; the unclean shall not pass over it ; but it shall be for those : · the wayfaring men, though fools, shall not err therein.

No lion shall be there, nor any ravenous beast shall go up thereon, it shall not be found there ; but the redeemed shall walk there :

And the ransomed of the Lord shall return, and come to Zion with songs and everlasting joy upon their heads : they shall obtain joy and gladness, and sorrow and sighing shall flee away.

Then shall the congregation kneel :

PRAYERS OF THANKSGIVING

Let us pray

ETERNAL Father, Judge of the Nations, we come before thee in gratitude and praise, in humility and faith, to give thee hearty thanks for thy mercy shewn us in the victory granted to our arms and those of our Allies.

O ALMIGHTY God, the Sovereign Commander of all the world, in whose hand is power and might which none is able to withstand : We bless and magnify thy great and glorious Name for this happy Victory, the whole glory whereof we do ascribe to thee, who art the only giver of Victory. And, we beseech thee, give us grace to improve this great mercy to thy glory, the advancement of thy Gospel, the honour of our Sovereign, and, as much as

· 4

in us lieth, to the good of all mankind. And, we beseech thee, give us such a sense of this great mercy, as may engage us to a true thankfulness, such as may appear in our lives by an humble, holy, and obedient walking before thee all our days, through Jesus Christ our Lord ; to whom with thee and the Holy Spirit, as for all thy mercies, so in particular for this Victory and Deliverance, be all glory and honour, world without end. Amen.

O ETERNAL God, the disposer and judge of nations, we bless thy holy Name for the steadfast support of all the communities of the Commonwealth and Empire who have joined with us against the enemy ; we remember with thanksgiving that with one purpose and will they stood together to resist the tyrant and oppressor and, with one heart and mind, fought that freedom and justice might not perish from the earth. We give thanks for their valour and for the manifold benefits which we enjoyed through the counsel, support and sacrifice of their Governments and peoples. We pray that thy blessing may rest upon all the nations and lands over which thou hast called thy servant GEORGE to be King, so that with steadfast minds we may in harmony and fellowship fulfil thy righteous purposes and promote the good of all men. O Lord save thy people and bless thine inheritance ; through Jesus Christ our Lord. Amen.

Then shall the Congregation join together in saying :

THE GENERAL THANKSGIVING

A LMIGHTY God, Father of all mercies, we thine unworthy servants do give thee most humble and hearty thanks for all thy goodness and lovingkindness to us and to all men. We bless thee for our creation, preservation, and all the blessings of this life ; but above all, for thine inestimable love in the redemption of the world by our Lord Jesus Christ ; for the means of grace, and for the hope of glory. And, we beseech thee, give us that due sense of all thy mercies, that our hearts may be unfeignedly thankful, and that we shew forth thy praise, not only with our lips, but in our lives ; by giving up ourselves to thy service, and by walking before thee in holiness and righteousness all our days ; through Jesus Christ our Lord, to whom with thee and the Holy Ghost be all honour and glory, world without end. Amen.

N OW unto him that is able to do exceeding abundantly above all that we ask or think, according to the power that worketh in us, unto him be glory in the Church, by Christ Jesus throughout all ages, world without end. Amen.

5

Then follows the PSALM OF PRAISE XCVI

O SING unto the Lord a new song : sing unto the Lord, all the whole earth.
 Sing unto the Lord, and praise his Name : be telling of his salvation from day to day.

Declare his honour unto the heathen : and his wonders unto all people.

For the Lord is great, and cannot worthily be praised : he is more to be feared than all gods.

As for all the gods of the heathen, they are but idols : but it is the Lord that made the heavens.

Glory and worship are before him : power and honour are in his sanctuary.

Ascribe unto the Lord, O ye kindreds of the people : ascribe unto the Lord worship and power.

Ascribe unto the Lord the honour due unto his Name : bring presents, and come into his courts.

O worship the Lord in the beauty of holiness : let the whole earth stand in awe of him.

Tell it out among the heathen that the Lord is King : and that it is he who hath made the round world so fast that it cannot be moved ; and how that he shall judge the people righteously.

Let the heavens rejoice, and let the earth be glad : let the sea make a noise, and all that therein is.

Let the field be joyful, and all that is in it : then shall all the trees of the wood rejoice before the Lord.

For he cometh, for he cometh to judge the earth : and with righteousness to judge the world, and the people with his truth.

GLORIA

THE SERMON

BY THE

LORD ARCHBISHOP OF CANTERBURY

HYMN

AND did those feet in ancient time
 Walk upon England's mountains green ?
And was the holy Lamb of God
 On England's pleasant pastures seen ?

And did the Countenance Divine
 Shine forth upon our clouded hills ?
And was Jerusalem builded here
 Among these dark Satanic Mills ?

6

Bring me my Bow of burning gold ;
Bring me my Arrows of desire :
Bring me my Spear : O Clouds unfold !
Bring me my Chariot of fire !

I will not cease from Mental Fight,
Nor shall my Sword sleep in my hand
Till we have built Jerusalem
In England's green and pleasant Land.

PRAYERS OF SUPPLICATION

Let us pray

Lord, have mercy upon us.
Christ, have mercy upon us.
Lord, have mercy upon us.

OUR Father, which art in heaven, Hallowed be thy Name. Thy kingdom come. Thy will be done, in earth as it is in heaven. Give us this day our daily bread. And forgive us our trespasses, As we forgive them that trespass against us. And lead us not into temptation ; But deliver us from evil : For thine is the kingdom, The power, and the glory, For ever and ever. Amen.

WE confess to thee with our whole heart our neglect and forgetfulness of thy commandments ; our wrong doing, speaking and thinking ; the hurt we have done to others and the good we have left undone. O God, forgive thy people that have sinned against thee, and blot out all our transgressions ; through Jesus Christ our Lord. Amen.

O LORD God of our fathers, who in thy goodness hast led this people hitherto by wondrous ways, who makest the nations to praise thee, and knittest them together in the bonds of peace ; We beseech thee to pour thy blessing on the Empire over which thou hast called thy servant GEORGE to be King. Grant that all, of whatsoever race or tongue, may in prosperity and peace be united in the bond of brotherhood, and in the one fellowship of the Faith, so that we may be found a people acceptable unto thee, through Jesus Christ our Lord. Amen.

WE commend, O Lord God, into the arms of thy mercy those who have died in the service of their country : beseeching for them thy Son's blessing upon all who lay down their life for their friends, and the immortal crown of the faithful who overcome : through Jesus Christ our Lord.

7

117

EVERLASTING Father, we commend to thee those for whom the end of the war is not the end of suffering, the wounded, the homeless, the hungry, the bereaved.

WE pray for the leaders and peoples of the United Nations ; for the restoration of order, health and civilian life throughout the world : and for our enemies in defeat that thou wilt have pity on them, shew them thy will, and turn their minds to justice, truth and peace.

ALMIGHTY God, from whom all thoughts of truth and peace proceed ; kindle, we pray thee, in the hearts of all men the true love of peace ; and guide with thy pure and peaceable wisdom those who take counsel for the nations of the earth : that in tranquillity thy kingdom may go forward, till the earth is filled with the knowledge of thy love, through Jesus Christ our Lord.   Amen.

HYMN

NOW thank we all our God,
　　With heart, and hands, and voices,
Who wondrous things hath done,
In whom his world rejoices ;
　Who from our mother's arms
　　Hath bless'd us on our way
　With countless gifts of love,
　　And still is ours to-day.

　O may this bounteous God
Through all our life be near us,
　With ever joyful hearts
And blessèd peace to cheer us ;
　And keep us in his grace,
　　And guide us when perplex'd,
　And free us from all ills
　　In this world and the next.

　All praise and thanks to God
The Father now be given,
　The Son, and Him who reigns
With them in highest Heaven,
　The One Eternal God,
　　Whom earth and Heav'n adore,
　For thus it was, is now,
　　And shall be evermore.   Amen.

8

During the singing of the Hymn, the Archbishop and the Dean and Chapter take their places before the Altar.

Then is the TE DEUM solemnly sung, all standing.

TE DEUM LAUDAMUS

WE praise thee, O God : we acknowledge thee to be the Lord.

All the earth doth worship thee : the Father everlasting.

To thee all Angels cry aloud : the Heavens, and all the Powers therein.

To thee Cherubin and Seraphin : continually do cry,

Holy, Holy, Holy : Lord God of Sabaoth ;

Heaven and earth are full of the majesty : of thy Glory.

The glorious company of the Apostles : praise thee

The goodly fellowship of the Prophets : praise thee.

The noble army of Martyrs : praise thee.

The holy Church throughout all the world : doth acknowledge thee ;

The Father : of an infinite Majesty ;

Thine honourable, true : and only Son ;

Also the Holy Ghost : the Comforter.

Thou art the King of Glory : O Christ.

Thou art the everlasting Son : of the Father.

When thou tookest upon thee to deliver man : thou didst not abhor the Virgin's womb.

When thou hadst overcome the sharpness of death : thou didst open the Kingdom of Heaven to all believers.

Thou sittest at the right hand of God : in the Glory of the Father.

We believe that thou shalt come : to be our Judge.

We therefore pray thee, help thy servants : whom thou hast redeemed with thy precious blood.

Make them to be numbered with thy Saints : in glory everlasting.

O Lord, save thy people : and bless thine heritage.

Govern them : and lift them up for ever.

Day by day : we magnify thee ;

And we worship thy Name : ever world without end.

Vouchsafe, O Lord : to keep us this day without sin.

O Lord, have mercy upon us : have mercy upon us.

O Lord, let thy mercy lighten upon us : as our trust is in thee.

O Lord, in thee have I trusted : let me never be confounded.

This being ended, the Congregation kneeling, shall be given

THE BLESSING

9

Then shall there sound a Fanfare from the West Gallery.

- THE NATIONAL ANTHEM

GOD save our gracious King !
Long live our noble King !
God save the King !
Send him victorious,
Happy and glorious,
Long to reign over us ;
God save the King !

O Lord our God, arise,
Scatter his enemies,
And make them fall.
Confound their politics,
Frustrate their knavish tricks,
On thee our hopes we fix ;
God save us all !

Thy choicest gifts in store
On him be pleased to pour ;
Long may he reign !
May he defend our laws,
And ever give us cause
To sing with heart and voice,
God save the King !

During the Retirement of Their Majesties, the Band plays.

Appendix C: Service Sheet for Anthony Powell's Funeral Service, Holy Trinity, Chantry, 4 April 2000

HOLY TRINITY CHURCH
Chantry

ANTHONY DYMOKE POWELL C.H. C.B.E.

21st December 1905 – 28th March 2000

Tuesday, 4th April, 2000

ORGAN PRELUDE
Jesu joy of man's desiring   J.S. Bach

THE SENTENCES

WELCOME AND PRAYER

HYMN

Guide me, O thou great Jehovah,
Pilgrim through this barren land;
I am weak, but thou art mighty,
Hold me with thy powerful hand:
Bread of heaven,
Feed me till I want no more.

2. Open now the crystal fountain,
Whence the healing stream doth flow;
Let the fire and cloudy pillar
Lead me all my journey through:
Strong Deliverer,
Be thou still my strength and shield.

3. When I tread the verge of Jordan,
Bid my anxious fears subside;
Death of death, and hell's Destruction,
Land me safe on Canaan's side:
Songs of praises
I will ever give to thee.

READING
Ezekiel 37

PSALM 91

He that dwelleth in the secret place of the most High shall abide under the shadow of the Almighty.

2 I will say of the Lord, He is my refuge and my fortress: my God; in him will I trust.

3 Surely he shall deliver thee from the snare of the fowler, and from the noisome pestilence.

4 He shall cover thee with his feathers, and under his wings shalt thou trust: his truth shall be thy shield and buckler.

5 Thou shalt not be afraid for the terror by night; nor for the arrow that flieth by day;

6 Nor for the pestilence that walketh in darkness; nor for the destruction that wasteth at noonday.

7 A thousand shall fall at thy side, and ten thousand at thy right hand; but it shall not come nigh thee.

8 Only with thine eyes shalt thou behold and see the reward of the wicked.

9 Because thou hast made the Lord, which is my refuge, even the
most High, thy habitation;

10 There shall no evil befall thee, neither shall any plague come nigh
thy dwelling.

11 For he shall give his angels charge over thee, to keep thee in all thy
ways.

12 They shall bear thee up in their hands, lest thou dash thy foot
against a stone.

13 Thou shalt tread upon the lion and adder: the young lion and the
dragon shalt thou trample under feet.

14 Because he hath set his love upon me, therefore will I deliver him: I
will set him on high, because he hath known my name.

15 He shall call upon me, and I will answer him: I will be with him in
trouble; I will deliver him, and honour him.

16 With long life will I satisfy him, and show him my salvation.

HYMN

My Soul, there is a Countrie
  Far beyond the stars,
Where stands a winged Sentrie
  All skilfull in the wars,

There above noise, and danger
  Sweet peace sits crown'd with smiles,
And one born in a Manger
  Commands the Beauteous files,

He is thy gracious friend,
  And (O my Soul awake!)
Did in pure love descend
  To die here for thy sake,

If thou canst get but thither,
  There growes the flowre of peace,
The Rose that cannot wither,
  Thy fortresse, and thy ease;

Leave then thy foolish ranges;
  For none can thee secure,
But one, who never changes,
  Thy God, thy life, thy Cure.

READING
Revelation 21: 1-7

PRAYERS

Lord, have mercy upon us.
Christ, have mercy upon us.
Lord, have mercy upon us.

Our Father, who art in heaven. Hallowed be thy name: Thy kingdom come; Thy will be done; On earth as it is in heaven. Give us this day our daily bread. And forgive us our trespasses. As we forgive those who trespass against us. And lead us not into temptation; But deliver us from evil. For thine is the kingdom, the power, and the glory, for ever and ever. Amen.

Minister: Enter not into judgement with thy servant, O Lord;
Answer: For in thy sight shall no man living be justified.
Minister: Grant unto him eternal rest;
Answer: And let perpetual light shine upon him.
Minister: We believe verily to see the goodness of the Lord;
Answer: In the land of the living.
Minister: O Lord, hear our prayer;
Answer: And let our day come unto thee.

READING

from

A Dance to the Music of Time

HYMN

Glorious things of thee are spoken,
Sion, city of our God!
He whose word cannot be broken
Formed thee for his own abode:
On the Rock of Ages founded,
What can shake thy sure repose?
With salvation's walls surrounded,
Thou may'st smile at all thy foes.

2. See, the streams of living waters,
Springing from eternal love,
Well supply thy sons and daughters,
And all fear of want remove:
Who can faint while such a river
Ever flows their thirst to assuage?
Grace, which like the Lord the Giver,
Never fails from age to age.

3. Saviour, if of Sion's city
I, through grace, a member am,
Let the world deride or pity,
I will glory in thy name:
Fading is the worldling's pleasure,
All his boasted pomp and show;
Solid joys and lasting treasure
None but Sion's children know.

THE BLESSING

This service sheet is reproduced by kind permission of John Powell.

Appendix D: Service Sheet for Anthony Powell's Memorial Service, Grosvenor Chapel, London, 4 May 2000

GROSVENOR CHAPEL
SOUTH AUDLEY STREET
LONDON W1

ANTHONY DYMOKE POWELL
CH CBE

21 December 1905–28 March 2000

11.30 AM THURSDAY 4 MAY 2000

ORGAN PRELUDE
'Nimrod' from *Enigma Variations* by Sir Edward Elgar

INTRODUCTION AND PRAYERS
The Reverend Simon Hobbs

HYMN

Immortal, invisible, God only wise,
In light inaccessible hid from our eyes,
Most blessed, most glorious, the ancient of days,
Almighty, victorious, thy great name we praise.

Unresting, unhasting, and silent as light,
Nor wanting, nor wasting, thou rulest in might;
Thy justice like mountains high soaring above,
Thy clouds which are fountains of goodness and love.

To all life thou givest, to both great and small;
In all life thou livest, the true life of all;
We blossom and flourish as leaves on the tree,
And wither and perish; but nought changeth thee.

Great Father of glory, pure Father of light,
Thine angels adore thee, all veiling their sight;
All laud we would render: O help us to see
'Tis only the splendour of light hideth thee.

LESSON
Ezekiel, Chapter 37, verses 1-14
Read by Harold Pinter

PSALM
Number 67

God be merciful unto us, and bless us; and shew us the light of his
countenance, and be merciful unto us;
    That thy way may be known upon earth: thy saving health among
all nations.
    Let the people praise thee, O God: yea, let all the people praise thee.
    O let the nations rejoice and be glad: for thou shalt judge the folk

righteously, and govern the nations upon earth.

Let the people praise thee, O God: let all the people praise thee.

Then shall the earth bring forth her increase: and God, even our own God, shall give us his blessing.

God shall bless us: and all the ends of the world shall fear him.

READING

From *The Garden of Proserpine* by A.C. Swinburne
Emma Fielding

ANTHEM

Ave Maria Stella by Edvard Grieg

HYMN

Let all the world in every corner sing,
My God and King!
The heav'ns are not too high,
His praise may thither fly;
The earth is not too low,
His praises there may grow.
Let all the world in every corner sing,
My God and King!

Let all the world in every corner sing,
My God and King!
The Church with psalms must shout,
No door can keep them out;
But above all the heart
Must bear the longest part.
Let all the world in every corner sing,
My God and King!

THE ADDRESS

Hugh Massingberd

MUSIC

Nocturne No. 4 in F by Frederic Chopin
Played by Christopher Ross

READING
From *Measure for Measure* by William Shakespeare
Jonathan Cecil

SONG
If You Were the Only Girl in the World
Music by Nat D. Ayer Lyrics by Clifford Grey
Sung by Karl Daymond

READING
From *A Dance to the Music of Time* by Anthony Powell
Simon Russell Beale

PRAYERS AND BLESSING

HYMN

Guide me, O thou great Jehovah,
  Pilgrim through this barren land;
I am weak, but thou art mighty,
  Hold me with thy powerful hand;
    Bread of heaven,
Feed me till I want no more.

Open now the crystal fountain,
  Whence the healing stream doth flow;
Let the fire and cloudy pillar
  Lead me all my journey through:
    Strong Deliverer,
Be thou still my strength and shield.

When I tread the verge of Jordan,
  Bid my anxious fears subside;
Death of death, and hell's Destruction,
  Land me safe on Canaan's side:
    Songs of praises
I will ever give to thee.

MUSIC
From *Carmen* by Georges Bizet

Appendix E: Rhythms of Dance

An Illustrated talk for the Anthony Powell Society by Paul Guinery, at the
Swedenborg Society, Bloomsbury Way, London, WC1, 26 February 2007.

RHYTHMS OF DANCE
An illustrated talk for the Anthony Powell Society

The Swedenborg Society, Bloomsbury, London, WC1

26 February 2007

*This talk arose from an invitation the Society's Chairman, Patric Dickinson,
extended to me and which, as a long-standing admirer of Powell's works as
well as an enthusiast for the popular music of his era, I was delighted to
accept. But I really must acknowledge two "sources" for my material: Hilary
Spurling's invaluable listing of musical references in her handbook* Invitation
to the Dance *and an excellent article by John Monagan,* "Dance Music", *in
the centenary issue of the Anthony Powell Society* Newsletter *(21, Winter
2005). I've plundered both sources shamelessly. What follows is very much
in the nature of notes I made for my original talk, which was also delivered
somewhat* ad hoc. *I've not attempted to make it more "literary" so
allowances should be made for its informal style.*

Good evening. John Monagan points out that music wasn't really one of
Anthony Powell's interests and mentions the writer's own acknowledgement,
in his memoirs *To Keep the Ball Rolling*, that he had "no musical
sensitivities". He also refers to Kingsley Amis's account of Amis trying to
play for Powell a recording of music by Constant Lambert, one of the models
for the character of the composer Hugh Moreland. After the first record,
Powell fell asleep.

I'm going to begin with one of the earliest musical references in *Dance*.
About thirty pages into *A Question of Upbringing* there's a mention of a song
called *Dapper Dan*: it crops up in a conversation between the schoolboys
Jenkins, Templer and Stringham after the raffish Templer has got back from a
visit to London, ostensibly to have his eyes tested; in fact he's been occupying
himself in a much more gratifying way. The sardonic Stringham remarks

> *my dear Peter, why do you always go about dressed as if you were
> going to dance up and down a row of naked ladies singing "Dapper
> Dan was a very handy man" or something equally lyrical? You get
> more like an advertisement for gents' tailoring every day.*

Dapper Dan is an aptly topical reference because it dates from 1921, around
the year *Dance* opens: the number came from a revue at the Prince of Wales'
Theatre called *A to Z* and which mostly had a score by Ivor Novello. A young

Gertrude Lawrence appeared in it – as did Jack Buchanan whom we'll hear in a moment along with a pair of American sisters, Helen and Josephine Trix. Sister acts were very popular in the 1920s – there were also the Dolly Sisters and the Duncan Sisters – later on, in the '40s, came the Andrews Sisters. The song was an interpolation by the team of Albert von Tilzer and Lew Brown called *Dapper Dan, the Sheik of Alabam* and was originally introduced in the States in a Broadway revue called *The Midnight Rounders* by Eddie Cantor. Jack Buchanan and the Trix Sisters send up the number: in the spoken introduction on the record (rather hard to hear) Buchanan, when asked to sing an American song, says he knows "all three" and that he'll "lay 6 to 4 that Dapper Dan comes from Dixie". Dan works for the railways as a Pullman porter and seems to get around the network of the Deep South with admirable thoroughness. If it's not exactly a question of a girl in every port, then at least there's a girl waiting at every station.

Here's the first chorus of the song:

> *If I lose my gal in Tennessee, that won't worry me,*
> *„Cause I've got another honey lamb,*
> *Waitin' for me down in Alabam.*
> *And If I lose my gal in Alabam, I won't feel blue,*
> *„Cause I've got one in Georgia,*
> *That I can march right to.*
> *If I lose my gal in Georgia, bet that I won't pine,*
> *„Cause I've got another mamma waiting,*
> *Down in sunny Caroline.*
> *Now I ain't handsome, I ain't sweet,*
> *But I've got a brand of lovin' that can't be beat,*
> *I'm the ladies' man, Dapper Dan from Dixieland.*

DAPPER DAN

Jack Buchanan / The Trix Sisters / 1921

Later on in the sequence, though still during the 1920s, there's a description in *A Buyer's Market* of the dance given by Lord and Lady Huntercombe at their house in Belgrave Square – the famous occasion when Barbara Goring empties the contents of a sugar castor over Widmerpool. There are two parties going on that night – the alternative is at the Spanish Embassy on the other side of the square – with competing dance bands. At the Huntercombes', one of the tunes their band is playing is *The Blue Room* from one of the earliest successful musical comedies by Richard Rodgers and Lorenz Hart: *The Girl Friend*. Produced on Broadway in 1926, it has a ludicrous plot about a man attempting to win a bicycle race and lead his sweetheart to the altar whilst fighting off a bunch of crooked gamblers who are attempting to nobble his chances on two wheels. The show transferred to London in 1927 when the entire plot was ditched in favour of a bedroom farce called *Kitty's Kisses* (bicycling was not considered by the producers a suitably English sport) – it was a big success and ran a year at the Palace Theatre. Quite a lot of the original score was also scrapped but not one of the plum songs, *The Blue Room*. It's one of those numbers that often crop up in 1920s and 1930s musicals in which the hero and heroine dream fondly of their future "love nest" together.

Powell has a nice description of Widmerpool dancing at the Huntercombes' – not a man to be exactly light on his feet but *ploughing his way round the room, as if rowing a dinghy in rough water.*

THE BLUE ROOM

Fred Rich & his Orchestra (with Red Nichols, cornet) / May 1926

At the Opening of *Casanova's Chinese Restaurant,* in what might be called a "flash-forward" rather than a "flash-back", Nicholas Jenkins finds himself on the site of the bombed-out pub in Gerrard Street where he and Moreland used to drink before the war and where they first heard a blonde street-singer on crutches rendering *Pale Hands I Loved: a Kashmiri Song.* Right on cue that same singer reappears, like some occult vision, to spur Jenkins's melancholic nostalgia. The ballad itself is by the composer Amy Woodforde-Finden, born in 1860. She was English, but was born in Valparaiso, in Chile, and she later married an officer in the Indian Army – so obviously she had some experience of Kashmir. Originally she couldn't find a publisher for her four *Indian Love Lyrics* (*Pale Hands* is the third in the set) so had them privately printed; a singer called Hamilton Earle took up the songs and made them so popular that Boosey & Hawkes, the publishers of ballad songs at the turn of the century, brought them out in 1902. Amy Woodforde-Finden went on (and on) writing exotic song cycles with titles such as *A Lover in Damascus, Little Japanese Songs, A Dream of Egypt, Stars of the Desert, The Pagoda of Flowers etc.* All of them deeply unfashionable today.

In *Dance* Moreland is characteristically sardonic about *Pale Hands I Loved Beside the Shalimar:* discussing with Jenkins

> the whereabouts of the Shalimar, and why the locality should have been the haunt of pale hands and those addicted to them.

> *"A nightclub, do you think?" Moreland had said. "A bordel,*
> *perhaps. Certainly an establishment catering for exotic tastes –*
> *and I suspect not very healthy ones either. How I wish there were*
> *somewhere like that where we could spend the afternoon Why did*
> *they dwell* <u>on</u> *the cool waters? I can't understand the proposition.*
> *Where they in a boat?...*

> *Perhaps this was a houseboat of ill fame ...*

Moreland goes on, with reference to a line in the lyric

> *"Whom do you lead on Rapture's roadway far?" What a pertinent*
> *question. But where can we go?*

Well, they decide against going to Casanova's Chinese Restaurant and end up drinking at Moreland's flat but not before he himself has offered his own rendition, in the street, of the song *as loudly trilled by his aunt* from Fulham.

In the same vein as that no doubt shaky version, I'm offering something equally dodgy, vocally, by a most unlikely singer: not in this case a woman, but the sexually ambiguous film-star of the silent era, Rudolph Valentino whose premature death in 1926 prompted a commemorative song with the apt title of *There's a New Star in Heaven Tonight* ... Unlike his screen rival Ramon Novarro, who had a very good baritone voice, Valentino couldn't really sing but made a record for the Brunswick recording company in 1923 which was only issued after his death.

There's a further reference to the song at the end of *The Kindly Ones* and it's made by Moreland in connection with his love for the actress Matilda Wilson or "Matty" as he calls her. He quotes the lines *Whom do you lead on Rapture's roadway far, before you agonize them in farewell?* with reference to Matilda leaving him for Sir Magnus Donners.

PALE HANDS I LOVED

Rudolph Valentino / unknown orchestra / 1923

Next, something to recall that "hostess with the mostest" Molly Jeavons. Well-born sister of Jumbo, Earl of Ardglass and Katherine, Lady Warminster, she married firstly John, Lord Sleaford, the uncle of Chips Lovell; secondly, Ted Jeavons. In the fourth novel of the sequence, *At Lady Molly's,* Chips tells Jenkins that Molly married Lord Sleaford *straight from the ballroom. She was only eighteen. Never seen a man before.* And Chips goes on to say that if Lord Sleaford hadn't died during the great epidemic of Spanish 'flu, in

1918, *she would still be – in the words of an Edwardian song my father hums whenever her name is mentioned – "Molly the Marchioness".*

Molly the Marchioness comes from a musical comedy of 1902 called *A Country Girl* which was a huge hit in its day. (Interestingly enough, another successful show produced that same year was called *My Lady Molly.*). It ran for over two years at Daly's theatre, now demolished, but which stood at the north-east corner of Leicester Square and the show had music by two of the outstanding composers of the period, Lionel Monckton and Paul Rubens. At one point, there were five separate companies touring the show in Britain; it also went out to the Empire: to South Africa and Australia; and reached Broadway in 1911. A young Anthony Powell might even have seen a production of the show himself, because it was revived in London in 1914 and again in 1931.

A Country Girl has its first act set in Devon and the characters include Geoffrey Challoner, the impoverished lord of the manor, and his servant Barry; Sir Joseph Verity, his new tenant of the house, who's trying to get his son Douglas into parliament; an Indian Rajah, who's actually Mr Quinton Raikes in disguise: he fictitiously fell off a mountain in India but faked the "accident" in order to get away from his domineering wife, an Indian Princess; and Marjorie Joy, the "country girl" of the title, who's done well for herself as a singer. In the second act the entire cast decamps to Mayfair for a ball at the house of Lord Anchester in which Barry now dresses, for no well-explained reason, as an elderly lady. At one point, the "country girl", who seems to be getting ideas above her station, is told the cautionary tale of "Molly the Marchioness" who was once simple Molly Gurney from Little Witticombe before she married a lord from London. So in that sense the song doesn't really fit with Molly Jeavons's own background. But it would have been topical for a show of this period, in that a number of fairly humble young ladies of the theatre (the Gaiety Girls in particular) did end up marrying into the aristocracy.

The number was apparently recorded in 1902 by its original performer, Evie Greene, a stalwart *comedienne* of the Edwardian musical stage, but it was never issued. So I shall render it for you ...

MOLLY THE MARCHIONESS

There's an interesting link between *Molly the Marchioness* and the next song, which I'm going to introduce by reading a section from *At Lady Molly's:* it's at the point where Ted Jeavons is reminiscing about his time on leave in London during the First World War and he says:

> *Didn't know a soul. Not a bloody cat. Well, after I'd had a bit of a*
> *lie-up in bed, I thought I'd go to a show. The MO had told me to*
> *look in on Daly's, if I got the chance. It was a jolly good piece of*
> *advice. <u>The Maid of the Mountains</u>. Top-hole show. José Collins.*
> *She married into the aristocracy like myself, but that's nothing to*
> *do with the story. I bought myself a stall, thinking I might catch a*
> *packet in the next ,strafe' and never sit in a theatre again.*

Ted Jeavons goes on to describe how he caught sight of a nurse who gave him "the glad eye"; she turns out to be the Honourable Mildred Blaides, later Mrs Haycock, and he subsequently spends the rest of his leave with her.

The Maid of the Mountains was a phenomenally successful show of the war years: it ran nearly 1400 performances and only came off when its temperamental star, José Collins, got tired of appearing in it. Ted was right in thinking she did indeed marry into the aristocracy herself. The show has a comic-opera plot set amongst brigands on high terrain in southern Europe and concerns Teresa, the "maid of the mountains" and her love for her Chief, Baldassare. The book was by the distinguished playwright Frederick Lonsdale, with music mostly by Harold Fraser-Simson. *Love Will Find A Way* was the hit tune and here it is, sung by its original interpreter, José Collins in one of the cast-recordings made for Columbia in 1917.

LOVE WILL FIND A WAY

José Collins / Daly's Theatre Orchestra / 1917

One of Moreland's fascinations (shared also by me) is for the sound of the pianola playing popular music. In that same passage I quoted earlier from *Casanova's Chinese Restaurant* about the bombed-out pub, Powell writes:

> *a floorless angle of the wall to which a few lumps of plaster and*
> *strips of embossed paper still adhered, was all that remained of the*
> *alcove where we had sat, a recess which also enclosed the*
> *mechanical piano into which, periodically, Moreland would feed a*
> *penny to invoke one of those fortissimo tunes belonging to much the*
> *same period as the blonde singer's repertoire.*

Well, here's a splendid example of a pianola roll – certainly playing *fortissimo* if not strictly speaking a number from the Edwardian period. It's an Ampico roll (these were the Rolls-Royces of piano rolls because they had greater sensitivity in dynamic than their rivals) cut by Adam Carroll, a well-known pianola "performer" and it's a number by Jerome Kern: *Who?* from his 1925 musical comedy about a female circus performer, *Sunny*.

WHO?

Ampico piano roll, cut (in the 1920s) by Adam Carroll

We've heard popular music only so far, but I think we should redress the balance now with something more "serious". Hugh Moreland is the main musician pictured in *Dance*, though there are others. Constant Lambert is often cited as an inspiration for Moreland's character but I wouldn't want to press the point: I think many characters in Powell's cast-list are undoubtedly composite creations. But there are some salient correspondences between Lambert and Moreland: Lambert had early fame as the 22-year-old composer of *The Rio Grande* in 1927 and although he subsequently wrote a lot of very fine – and actually much more sophisticated – pieces of music, he never really achieved similar fame again. The piece became a bit of a millstone round his neck; he succumbed eventually to drink and despair, and died of undiagnosed diabetes at the age of only 46 in 1951. As well as sharing Moreland's *penchant* for public-houses, Lambert had a similarly wry sense of humour, writing a very witty book of music criticism called *Music Ho!* And he was also known to pen limericks, including one about the Bishop of Western Japan. Much of his time was spent as a ballet conductor; in fact he was on tour with Sadler's Wells Ballet in Holland in May 1940 when the Germans invaded the Low Countries. The company got trapped there and after a traumatic two days, barely managed to get away to England.

Two years later, in 1942, Lambert was able to recall this frightening period "in tranquillity" in a short orchestral piece which he called *Aubade Héroïque* – he said that it was "inspired by daybreak during the invasion of Holland, the calm of the surrounding park, contrasting with the distant mutterings of war".

The work was dedicated to Ralph Vaughan Williams on VW's 70th birthday.

CONSTANT LAMBERT: AUBADE HÉROÏQUE

English Northern Philharmonia / David Lloyd-Jones

Following that wartime piece, some other military associations. In *Books Do Furnish a Room*, the first of the post-war novels, Jenkins contrasts his own melancholy with the optimism of the period immediately after the First World War, summarized for him by a snatch of a tune Ted Jeavons liked to hum whenever he was in "poor form": *Après la guerre, there'll be a good time everywhere*. The song he's quoting comes from a revue called *Hullo,*

America! which starred the American singer Elsie Janis and opened right at
the end of war, at the Palace Theatre in September 1918. The show's
conductor, Herman Finck, wrote most of the songs – though *Après la Guerre*
was an interpolation by Basil Hilliam. It was originally sung (and recorded)
by the vocal quintet of Elsie Janis, Stanley Lupino, Owen Nares (a well-
known matinée idol), Maurice Chevalier and Will West. Elsie Janis was a big
American star, very strong singer of ragtime and jazz. The revue also
included numbers such as "Percy from Peckham" and "The Jazz Band" in
which Elsie Janis was joined by the Palace chorus girls wearing "Jazz"
dresses with skirts which parted to display the Stars and Stripes at the end of
the number.

A real craze for revue in London began around 1912: many of the shows were
full of the new American ragtime music – *Hullo, Ragtime!* (1912) was
followed by entertainments with titles such as *Hullo, Tango!, Business as
Usual* (1914), *Zig-Zag!, Joy-Bells!, Jig-Saw!, Keep Smiling, Not Likely, Bric-
à-Brac, Airs and Graces, Bubbles, Odds and Ends, Pell-Mell* - and, *Hullo,
America!* These played at big theatres such as the Palace, the Hippodrome,
the Alhambra and smaller stages such as the Ambassadors' and the
Vaudeville. A lot of the shows were spectacular – modelled on the Ziegfeld
Follies in New York – and became standard theatre-going fare for soldiers
"on leave" from the trenches who wanted to see something light and frothy,
with some comedy and plenty of pretty girls.

I couldn't find a recording of this so I'll try to render it myself.

APRES LA GUERRE

Now one of the great songs of the First World War: *There's a Long, Long
Trail A-Winding.* At the end of *The Kindly Ones,* Ted Jeavons actually sings
this when Jenkins unexpectedly meets his brother Stanley Jeavons who offers
to fix his call-up and commission after Widmerpool has been so unhelpful.

> *Jeavons moved towards the table where the beer bottles stood.
> Suddenly he began to sing in that full, deep, unexpectedly attractive
> voice, so different from the croaking tones in which he ordinarily
> conversed.*

After this "performance", Jeavons says

> *Used to sing that while we were blanco-ing ... God, how fed up I
> got cleaning that bloody equipment.*

The song became so associated with the "Tommies in the trenches" that it's a bit of a surprise to realize that it was in fact written before the war (in 1913) by two American college students at Yale: James Reed and Zo Elliott, though it wasn't published at the time in the States. It did get into print, though, in England and became one of the great war-songs expressing the soldiers' longing for those left behind at home. This American recording dates from 1915, the year the song was re-imported back into the USA and is sung as a duet by tenor and baritone.

THERE'S A LONG, LONG TRAIL A-WINDING

James Reed & JF Harrison (Reed Miller & Fred Wheeler) / September 1915

By contrast, here's a song which became popular just before the Second World War: *South of the Border* by Jimmy Kennedy and Michael Carr and it's the one that Private Jones, D renders in the cave-like Welsh chapel called Sardis in *Valley of the Bones*:

> *suddenly at the far end of the cave, like the anthem of the soloist bursting gloriously from a hidden choir, a man's voice, deep throated and penetrating, sounded, rose, swelled in a lament of heartbreaking melancholy.*

Powell continues:

> *the message of the [Mission] bell, the singer's tragic tone announcing it, underlined life's inflexible call to order, reaffirming the illusory nature of love and pleasure. Even as the words trailed away, heavy steps sounded from the other end of the chapel, as if forces of authority were already on the move to effect the unhappy lover's expulsion from the Mission premises and delights of Mexico.*

This recording was made in May 1939.

SOUTH OF THE BORDER

Henry Hall & his orchestra / vocal by Bob Mallin / May 1939

The vocal proclivities of the unpredictable Bracey are mentioned in *The Kindly Ones*. Bracey, you'll remember, was Jenkins's father's soldier-servant, described as "a man of unparalleled smartness of turnout, who looks like a fox-terrier and has what are known in the Jenkins household as his "funny days" when he gives way to melancholia. He's "sweet on" Bilson, the equally unpredictable parlour maid but is spurned by her and is killed on the retreat from Mons in 1914. When all is comparatively well with the world, Bracey likes to hum softly under his breath a music-hall number called *I Wish it was Sunday Night*. This was written by the music-hall artiste Billy Williams in collaboration with Fred Godrey and Hugo Trevor.

Billy Williams was known as "The Man in the Velvet Suit", one of his trademark costumes on the Halls. He was an Australian who came to London in 1906 and was one of the first to realise the potential of the gramophone, unlike some of his colleagues who were hostile to it. He recorded many of his numbers, such as *When Father Papered the Parlour* and *John, Go and Put Your Trousers On*; but he died at 37 in 1915. Here's his splendid recording of *I Wish It Was Sunday Night* from about 1912.

I WISH IT WAS SUNDAY NIGHT

Billy Williams / recorded 1912

We're told in *Dance* that Sir Magnus Donners, that formidable if somewhat enigmatic industrialist is fond of Wagner's opera *Parsifal* and sheds tears over the death of Liù, the slave-girl in Puccini's *Turandot*. Given his sexual proclivities, which are never quite specified by Powell who gives hints of masochistic tendencies involving young women for what would now be termed "bondage", the Puccini reference is not surprising. Liù, in the opera, is the slave-girl hopelessly in love with her master, the noble Calaf; he successfully solves the three riddles posed by the icy Turandot but agrees to forgo his reward and suffer death if she can only discover his name. Liù is the only one who knows it and is bound and tortured by Turandot's guards to make her reveal the secret (hence I think the appeal for Sir Magnus). She sings a heart-breaking appeal to the pitiless Princess and then, unable to bear any more pain, breaks free, seizes a dagger from one of the palace guards and stabs herself to death.

Here's what moved the lachrymatory ducts of that hard-bitten magnate: this version is sung by Mirella Freni.

DEATH OF LIU

Mirella Freni / Orchestra of Rome Opera House / Franco Ferraris

Still moving in the general area of sex in all its manifestations, here are two more representations of it. The character of the entertainer Heather Hopkins is amusingly drawn by Powell; she's described

as small, gnarled, dumpy, middle-aged; horn-rimmed spectacles and bulging blue flannel trousers; much addicted to barrack-room slang.

She's initially a friend of the lesbian couple Norah Tolland and Eleanor Walpole though she later drops them. She's also a night-club pianist who often accompanies Max Pilgrim.

It struck me that she had much in common with a between-the-wars entertainer called Gwen Farrar, though the latter was a cellist and a singer rather than a pianist. Gwen Farrar was a volcanic character who initially had a professional partnership with the pianist Norah Blaney until Norah married. Farrar then teamed up with the pianist and composer Billy Mayerl – disastrously, as it turned out. She was at times both unpredictable and unprofessional, often missing engagements to go drinking with her society friends (she really didn't need the money). When she wasn't playing the cello, she sang in a distinctly masculine voice, much admired by the lesbian coteries of the day.

Here she is with Billy Mayerl before their partnership broke up, in one of several records they made together. It's a satire, written and composed by the Weston Brothers, on the 1920s "flapper", recorded in 1928 and contrasts the pre-war girl with her modern counterpart. There are amusing lines such as "the old-fashioned girl was a plump-looking wench, when she'd got all her new bits-and-bobs on; the new-fashioned girl is so terribly thin, she looks like a gas-pipe with knobs on". The recording is introduced by Billy Mayerl with the warning to Gwen to "be careful".

OLD-FASHIONED GIRLS

Gwen Farrar / Billy Mayerl / 1928

The most memorable nightclub entertainer in *Dance* is Max Pilgrim and I think the models for his character are even clearer. Two names spring to my mind: Douglas Byng (whom we'll hear in incomparable action later on) and also Ronald Frankau who was a very popular cabaret artiste between the wars, often accompanied "at the piano" by Monte Crick. You'll recall the several references to the "suggestive songs" of Max Pilgrim in *Dance* – numbers such as "I'm Tess of Le Touquet, My Morals are Flukey"; "Heather, Heather, she's under the Weather"; and "Di, Di, in her collar and tie, quizzes the girls with her monocled eye". Ronald Frankau's material was more sophisticated than that and he was always immaculately dressed in tails, although of course we only have the evidence of the "cleaned-up" versions of his songs as they're the ones he recorded. The performances he gave in cabaret would doubtless have been "smuttier". He's still funny to listen to and here he is, in characteristic vein, with a 1933 recording called *Everyone's Got Sex-Appeal For Someone.*

EVERYONE'S GOT SEX-APPEAL FOR SOMEONE

Ronald Frankau / Monte Crick / October 1933

Music played a significant role during both major military conflicts of the last century, in a way that it no longer does: what memorable songs emerged from the Falklands War, for example? Here's another nostalgic Second World War song, mentioned by Powell in *The Valley of Bones* as being sung by Corporal Gwylt on his night out with the barmaid Maureen at Castlemallock. Jenkins and Roland Gwatkin eavesdrop on his performance which comes as a bombshell to the latter who's in love with Maureen himself. This is the song they hear, *popular* Jenkins comments *among the men on account of its nostalgic tones and rhythm.* It's called *Arm in Arm Together,* written by Church & Bradbury, and here's the version made by Ambrose and his orchestra, with the vocalist Jack Cooper, in March 1940.

ARM IN ARM

Ambrose and his orchestra / vocal by Jack Cooper / 1940

Now for a Classic of the First World War and a song that had a special resonance for Anthony Powell: he asked for it to be sung at his memorial service at Grosvenor Chapel in March 2000. It's also rendered, unexpectedly, by Ted Jeavons on the night of his reunion with Mrs Haycock at Dicky Umfraville's night-club in *At Lady Molly's*: when the band stops playing Ted suddenly breaks into *If You Were the Only Girl in the World* and follows it up with some rather melancholic reflections on the loss of innocence and illusions post-1918.

The song is one of the great ones from the First World War: many a soldier on leave must have heard it at the old Alhambra Theatre in Leicester Square during the run of *The Bing Boys Are Here* – a show that was more of a revue than a musical – in 1916. It was a huge success and gave birth to two sequels,

all with music by an American composer who'd settled over here, Nat D
Ayer. It was originally sung by the female star of the show, Violet Lorraine,
and the male comic, George Robey. Here's their original recording from
April 1916 which may not display the heights of singing technique but has
seldom been surpassed in terms of sheer poignancy. It's the one Powell
himself requested.

IF YOU WERE THE ONLY GIRL IN THE WORLD

Violet Lorraine / George Robey / 1916

I began with one of the tunes that drifted across Belgrave Square on that early
summer night in 1928 or '29 on the occasion of the Huntercombes' ball. The
other number from the nearby band at the Spanish Embassy which competed
with it, was also written by Rodgers and Hart. It's *Mountain Greenery*,
originally part of their score for the 1926 edition of the *Garrick Gaieties* in
New York and subsequently imported over here into the British version of
The Girl Friend in 1927. I'm going to attempt to play and sing it for you.

MOUNTAIN GREENERY

Earlier, I mentioned Douglas Byng as a possible model for Max Pilgrim.
Byng wrote a very entertaining book of *Reminiscences* in the 1970s looking
back over his career: like Max Pilgrim, he made his name as a performer of
his own material in cabarets. But he was much more than that: he was a very
accomplished performer who was a renowned Pantomime Dame; he also
contributed to many of the CB Cochran revues of the 1920s and appeared in
Noël Coward's revue *On With the Dance* and Cole Porter's musical *Wake Up
and Dream* – and, incidentally, introduced Porter's song "Miss Otis Regrets"
in the revue *Hi-Diddle-Diddle* in 1934. In fact his career lasted from 1917
right up until the 1960s. He was banned whenever possible by the BBC for
his "suggestiveness" though they relented enough to give him a 90th birthday
tribute in 1983, four years before he died.

One of his best-known "saucy" numbers of the 1930s was called *I'm a Tree*
and here's "Dougie" Byng, as he was affectionately known, performing it in a
relatively modern recording, which means we probably get more of the
original cabaret version than we would do from his period "cleaned-up for the
gramophone" version. It's prefaced by his own introduction which gives you
a very good flavour of what he was all about.

I'M A TREE

Douglas Byng / recorded 1967 (?) from Alan Melville's *Before the Fringe* (?)

Time for something serious now: it evokes the Mozart musical party which Odo Stevens throws for his guests in his house near Regent's Park. It's a performance of Mozart's *Die Entführung auf dem Serail* (*The Seraglio*). One of the stand-in violinists there turns out to be the ageing Carolo who's in fact not from Italy but from the North Midlands. And here's a very beautiful aria from the opera: *Wie ein Liebchen hat gefunden* in which Osmin, the servant of Pasha Selim and the overseer of the Harem, reflects from experience that "a woman must be watched or who knows what will occur" – advice that many of the male characters of *Dance* would have done well to follow. The singer is the bass Alexander Kipnis.

THE SERAGLIO

Alexander Kipnis / Berlin State Opera / Erich Orthmann / April 1931

Next, another reflection on Love, albeit very different in style. It's again from the pen of Rodgers and Hart, a number originally written for CB Cochran's *London Pavilion Revue* of 1927 – or *One Dam' Thing After Another* so named because when a man was asked what the show was like, he replied "well, it's just one damn thing after another". The song is *My Heart Stood Still* and it's mentioned in *A Buyer's Market* as one of the tunes played at the notorious party of Mrs Andriadis where it's performed by

> *a hunchback wearing a velvet smoking-jacket, playing an accordion, writhing backwards and forwards as he attacked his instrument with demiurgic frenzy.*

I couldn't find a recording of it played on the accordion (you'll probably be glad to hear) so we'll just have to put up with the divine Jessie Matthews who first performed it in the show, accompanied, as on this 1927 recording, by Leslie Hutchinson, or "Hutch", then at the start of his career. (Douglas Byng was also in the same show, as was Max Wall; it ran seven months.)

At the start you'll hear Miss Matthews giving an alternative line to the published version of the song: instead of "all through my school days, I hated boys" she sings "in Heathfield school days" a reference to the upper-crust girls' school near Ascot. Interestingly enough, another version of this was sung in the original revue, as follows: *the boys at Harrow, would always say, that Cupid's arrow, couldn't fly my way.*

MY HEART STOOD STILL

Jessie Matthews / Leslie "Hutch" Hutchinson / October 1927

Powell must have had a fondness for Music Hall, judging by the number of references to it – though it was pretty much a dying art-form during his youth. In *The Soldier's Art* Sergeant Ablett, the NCO in charge of the Mobile Laundry Unit is singled out for one of his party-pieces *The Man Who Broke the Bank at Monte Carlo*. Ablett is described as looking like a veteran of Wellington's campaign and is a leading comedian at Divisional concert parties, his trouserless tap-dance a highly popular item; he's a great favourite with Stringham.

Here's a recording of the number (without the tap-dance) from the song's original creator, Charles Coborn whose other great number was *Two Lovely Black Eyes*. Coborn was born in 1852 and continued working the Halls for many years: *the Man who Broke the Bank* dates from 1891 and here's a wonderful recording he made of it rather later, in 1929, when he would have been aged 77.

THE MAN WHO BROKE THE BANK AT MONTE CARLO

Charles Coborn / 1929

Here's the number from just after the end of the First World War which is playing on the gramophone when Templer, Stringham and Jenkins visit a tea-shop as schoolboys in the summer of 1922 during the affair of "Braddock alias Thorne". It's called *Everything is Buzz-Buzz Now* from Charlot's revue *Buzz-Buzz* which opened at the Vaudeville Theatre in December 1918. The show had numbers such as *Coupons for Kisses, Winnie the Window Cleaner* (sung by a young Gertrude Lawrence); *Percy was Perfectly Priceless* and *The Corpse Reviver Rag.*

Everything is Buzz-Buzz Now was the finale to Act 1 and it has some amusing lyrics playing on the (then) new catch-phrase "buzz-buzz". I'll try to get the lyrics across to you at the piano as I couldn't find an original recording. Here are the first verse and chorus of the lyrics:

You've heard the latest phrase, it's going to be the craze,
It's buzz, buzz, buzz, buzz, buzz.
You buzz off to the city, you buzz off from your food,
You buzz into your office, say "buzz off!" if you're rude.
You buzz off out to dinner, and to the Hippodrome;
You buzz round after taxis and on a buzz-buzz home:

Chorus:
Everything is Buzz Buzz now! Everything is Buzz Buzz now!
You ring up on your "buzzer" and buzz with one anuzzer,
Or in other words, pow-wow.
Everything is Buzz Buzz now! Everything is Buzz somehow.
Now then, if you please, imitate the bees;
Everything is Buzz Buzz now!

EVERYTHING IS BUZZ-BUZZ NOW

Finally, just for fun, another "Max Pilgrim" song from Gwen Farrar and Billy Mayerl. It was a number satirising the confusion of the genders in the 1920s called *Masculine Women and Feminine Men* and it got them into trouble. It was rather risqué for its time with lyrics such as "sister is busy learning to shave, brother just loves his permanent wave" and Farrar had insisted on performing it with Mayerl during their act at the London Coliseum. But during a rehearsal, Sir Oswald Stoll, who built and managed the Coliseum, strongly objected to it as the Coliseum variety acts were meant to be something to which men could bring their wives and children *ie.* no blue material. Gwen Farrar told Billy Mayerl to take no notice and keep the number in the act. However, at the evening performance he struck up with another song whereupon she simply put her cello over her shoulder and walked off the stage. Afterwards, the audience were told that she'd felt ill and couldn't continue; in fact she went straight off to a club to drink with her friends. It wasn't quite the end of the Mayerl-Farrar partnership, but it wasn't long before they split up.

It's still a very amusing song even if you have to listen quite carefully to the words which aren't as clear as they might be on this recording from August 1926.

Masculine women, feminine men,
Which is the rooster, which is the hen?
It's hard to tell 'em apart today
...
Knickers and trousers, baggy and wide,

Nobody knows who's walking inside,
Those masculine women and feminine men!

It's as good a way as any to finish this foray into some of the potent "rhythms of *Dance*"

MASCULINE WOMEN AND FEMININE MEN

Gwen Farrar / Billy Mayerl / August 1926

Paul Guinery
February 2007, revised June 2007

© Paul Guinery, 2007

Appendix F: Soundtrack Music for Channel 4 TV Films of *Dance to the Music of Time*

Key:
Italics – TV film only
Bold Italics – Both novels and TV film
Bold – Discussed in entries above by name or first line of musical piece.
* Included on Soundtrack CD *A Dance to the Music of Time: Five Decades of Decadence* (Channel 4 / MCI MPRCD-002)

Episode 1. The Twenties

* *20th century Blues (opening credits, 1932 recording by Noel Coward)*

* *Masculine Women and Feminine Men (1926 recording, Raymond Newton and Savoy Band)*

I Love My Baby (78 rpm record in background – Templer's car)

* *Oxford (background orchestral music by Carl Davis)*

* ***My Heart Stood Still (Huntercombe dance, vocal by Andrew Halliday)***

* ***The Blue Room: "We'll have a – Blue Room | New room for – two room" (Huntercombe dance, vocal by Andrew Halliday)***

The Merry Widow Waltz (Huntercombe dance)

* ***Mountain Greenery: "In a mountain greenery" (Huntercombe dance, vocal by Andrew Halliday)***

The Charleston (at coffee stall)

La Paloma (accordionist at Mrs Andriadis' party)

There Are Fairies At the Bottom of our Garden (Max Pilgrim sings at Mrs Andriadis' party)

I Get Ideas (accordionist at Mrs Andriadis' party)

* *It Had to be You (dance band at Mr Deacon's birthday party)*

Oh God Our Help in Ages Past (hymn at Mr Deacon's funeral)

* *The Affair Begins (background orchestral music by Carl Davis)*

Some One to Watch Over Me (on piano at Ritz)

End credits (background music by Carl Davis)

Episode 2. The Thirties

* My Heart Stood Still (opening credits 1930s style vocal by Andrew Halliday)

Kashmiri Song: Pale hands I loved beside the Shalimar (blonde street singer vocal outside pub)

These Foolish Things (dance band at Umfraville's club)

Just One of Those Things (dance band at Umfraville's club)

I Get a Kick Out of You (dance band at Umfraville's club)

Dancing in the Dark (dance band at Umfraville's club)

I Wish It Was Sunday Night: "Monday, Tuesday, Wednesday, Thursday | May be merry and bright" (sung softly by Sergeant Bracey)

* Ghosts (background music by Carl Davis)

* Moreland's Piano Concerto (written for film score by Carl Davis)

Unidentified organ music at Uncle Giles' funeral

* Anything Goes (end credits, dance band arrangement of Cole Porter song)

Episode 3. The War Years

* It's a Lovely Day Tomorrow (opening and end credits, 1940 recording of vocal by Vera Lynn)

* Kiss Me Goodnight, Sergeant Major (1939 recording of vocal by Arthur Askey)

Conga (dance band at Café de Madrid)

As Time Goes By (dance band at Café de Madrid)

* Whitehall (background music by Carl Davis)

* Thanks, Mr Roosevelt (1941 recording by Harry Leader and his band)

Two pieces of piano music in background as Jenkins and Duport talk at Ritz Hotel: the first is Room Five-Hundred-and-Four (words by Eric Maschwitz and music by George Posford, written for the 1940 West End revue New Faces); the second is That Lovely Weekend (a 1941 popular song by Moira and Ted Heath, recorded by several artists, including Vera Lynn)

Bésame Mucho (played by dance band in Cairo night club as Widmerpool dances with Pamela)

* Waltz of my Heart (background music played by chamber group at Embassy reception, composed by Ivor Novello / Christopher Hassall)

* Some Day I'll Find You (orchestral arrangement of Noel Coward song played in background at Embassy reception)

Land of Hope and Glory (played by military band at St Paul's Cathedral victory thanksgiving service)

Episode 4. Postwar, Fifties and Sixties

Memories Are Made of This (opening credits, vocal by Dean Martin)

* Death of a Novelist (background music by Carl Davis)

** **Abduction from the Seraglio (excerpts from Mozart opera, Die Entführung aus dem Serail)***

* Honours (background music by Carl Davis)

Do Wah Diddy Diddy (Manfred Mann rock song played in background as Widmerpool meets Murtlock in what looks like a Wimpey bar of 1970s vintage)

Chant by Murtlock cult group

* The Death of Widmerpool (background music by Carl Davis)

20th Century Blues (end credits, vocal by Marianne Faithful)

Source:
CD booklet for *A Dance to the Music of Time: Five Decades of Decadence, Original Soundtrack composed and conducted by Carl Davis* (indicated by * in above list); this list is also available on Anthony Powell Society website. Thanks to Joe Trenn of the Anthony Powell Society for providing a copy of the CD and booklet. Other music not on CD as identified from videotapes of TV series with the help of Paul Guinery.

Notes on Contributors

Nicholas Birns teaches in the Department of Literature, Eugene Lang College, New School University, specializing in nineteenth and twentieth century literature and in literary theory. His book *Understanding Anthony Powell* was published in 2004 by University of South Carolina Press. His book, *Theory After Theory: An Intellectual History of Literary Theory*, appeared in 2010 from Broadview Press. He writes frequently for scholarly and general interest periodicals and serves on a number of academic committees and boards.

Edwin Bock is Emeritus Professor of Political Science at the Maxwell Graduate School of Syracuse University. After military service, he lived in London from 1946-52 as a graduate student, Fulbright Fellow and Instructor at the LSE. During that period he lived in Chelsea where, like Nick Jenkins, he spent several lifetimes in cinema queues with attractive young women. In addition to academic writing, he recently wrote, directed and appeared as stage manager / narrator in a play entitled *Waiting for (Dr) Belkin or Four Anthony Powell Characters in Search of a Coincidence: A Therapeutic Entertainment in Three and One-Quarter Scenes*, first presented in New York (a few blocks off Broadway) in December 2008 by the Northeast (US) Anthony Powell Society Local Group's Noel-Poel-Players, with a repeat performance in September 2009 at the Fifth Biennial Anthony Powell Conference, Georgetown University, Washington, DC.

Paul Guinery is an Oxford-educated linguist and a pianist accredited by the Royal College of Music, where he also studied the organ and opera. Now a freelance broadcaster, he spent all his working life at the BBC, first as an announcer with BBC World Service and later specialising in music programmes for Radio 3. During that time, he presented regular lunchtime recitals from the former Concert Hall at Broadcasting House and – latterly – the Wigmore Hall. For many years he hosted the popular request programme *Your Concert Choice*; presented *Sacred and Profane* on Sunday mornings; and fronted *Choirworks*, a specialist strand for choral music. He was also closely associated with the BBC Symphony Orchestra as their regular announcer both at home and abroad on tour. He has also written and presented many programmes about individual composers reflecting his diverse interests – from Delius to Irving Berlin, César Franck to Cole Porter. In February 2007 he wrote and presented a live performance entitled *Rhythms of Dance*: *An Illustrated talk for the Anthony Powell Society* at the Swedenborg Society, Bloomsbury Way, London, WC1, in which he performed many of the songs mentioned in Powell's novels.

John Gould was for 26 years an instructor in English literature and writing at Phillips Academy, Andover, Massachusetts, USA. During two of those years he taught a course in Anthony Powell's *A Dance to the Music of Time*. He has published a novel, a memoir, two cookbooks, a grammar textbook and, most recently, edited a collection of essays by his students, *Dance Class: American High School Students Encounter Anthony Powell's Dance to the Music of Time* (iUniverse Inc.; New York, NY and Bloomington, IN). Recently retired from teaching, he now lives north of Boston with his wife Jane and a cat.

Peter Kislinger is Lecturer in the Department of English at University of Vienna. His doctoral dissertation (Univ. of Vienna 1993) was "SOME TRUTHS SEEM ALMOST FALSEHOODS AND SOME FALSEHOODS ALMOST TRUTHS: Narrative technique, *mise-en-abymes*, intertextuality, constructive irony and the truth of fiction in Anthony Powell's *A Dance to the Music of Time*". Since 1993, freelance journalist for ORF / Radio Ö1 (writer, presenter and producer for various programmes, mainly in the music department) and for BBC Radio 4; articles for *Neue Zürcher Zeitung, Die Presse etc.*); main interests as a journalist: orchestral and chamber music from the UK and Nordic countries and live coverage from London of the *Last Night of the Proms* for ORF since 1997.

Jeffrey Manley lives in Bethesda, Maryland where he works as Senior Regulatory Advisor for United Airlines. He graduated from Harvard University with degrees in law and Russian studies. He is a frequent contributor to the Anthony Powell Society *Newsletter* and journal, *Secret Harmonies*, and to the *Evelyn Waugh Newsletter and Studies*. His knowledge of music is more extensive than Waugh's (who found listening to it painful) but less than Powell's (who seems to have listened to quite a lot of it and remembered much of what he heard).

Prue Raper trained for the theatre and as a singer before deciding to pursue a less risky profession, working in corporate communications for several major UK companies. However, being fortunate enough to have sympathetic bosses, she was able to continue to develop a professional singing career alongside her job. Since leaving office work, where she spent many years writing, she has continued to write and edit in a freelance capacity, as well as singing with professional choirs and as a soloist in the UK and abroad. Her devotion to Anthony Powell's work began in the early '60s; but on 4 May 2000, she was amazed and delighted to find herself quite unexpectedly singing in the choir at his Memorial Service in the Grosvenor Chapel. The other singers, never having heard of him, could not understand why she was so excited.

Anthony Powell Society Monographs

John S Monagan, *The Master and The Congressman* (2003)

Christine Berberich (ed.), *Writing about Anthony Powell: Perspectives on Writing about a Writer* (2005)

Jeffrey Manley *et al.*, *Dance Music: A Guide to Musical References in Anthony Powell's A Dance to the Music of Time* (2010)

Other Anthony Powell Society Publications

George Lilley & Keith C Marshall (eds), *Celebrating the 50th Anniversary of A Dance to the Music of Time: Proceedings of the First Biennial Anthony Powell Conference 2001* (2001)

George Lilley, Stephen Holden & Keith C Marshall (eds), *Anthony Powell and the Oxford of the 1920s: Proceedings of the Second Biennial Anthony Powell Conference 2003* (2004)

George Lilley & Keith C Marshall (eds), *Proceedings of the Anthony Powell Centenary Conference; Third Biennial Anthony Powell Conference 2005* (2007)

Powell throws into Dance *a huge variety of musical allusions, both classical and popular.*

This guide is most impressively researched; it is a fascinating and inestimable companion.

The guide gathers together a wealth of references, many identifiable but in danger of being forgotten; some tantalisingly allusive but now revealed in context. It fills in the background in a way I've found fascinating and from which I've learnt so much.

It will prove invaluable in years to come when the music of Powell's era will be even more underplayed and undervalued than it is nowadays, a decade after his death.

Jeff Manley has done a wonderful job keeping these musical references alive and preserving their meaning.

Paul Guinery

ISBN 978-0954173661

9 780954 173661